PENGUIN CLASSICS

THE PSALMS

The Book of Psalms is an ancient anthology of Hebrew songs and poems, thought to have been composed during the time of the Davidic monarchy (*c.* 1000 B.C. to its collapse in 586 B.C.). The psalms consist mainly of religious poems, hymns and prayers and songs of praise to God. Their authorship is for the most part unknown, and little is known of their history, but they probably formed part of the public worship of Israel. Ancient tradition makes King David the founder of the worship and the author of many of the psalms, as was his son and successor King Solomon (died *c.* 933 B. C.).

Peter Levi, a classical scholar, archaeologist and poet, was born in 1931. He has translated two books for the Penguin Classics, Pausanias' *Guide to Greece* (two volumes) and *The Psalms*, as well as a collection of Yevtushenko (with R. Milner-Gulland) for the Penguin Modern Poets. He has also edited Johnson's *A Journey to the Western Islands of Scotland* and Boswell's *The Journal of a Tour to the Hebrides* for the Penguin English Library and *The Penguin Book of Christian Verse* for The Penguin Poets. His book *The Light Garden of the Angel King*, an account of his travels in Afghanistan, is published in the Penguin Poetry Library. His most recent publication is *The History of Greek Literature* soon to be published by Penguin as *The Pelican History of Greek Literature*.

Peter Levi is Professor of Poetry in the University of Oxford.

Nicholas de Lange was born in 1944. He was formerly Parkes Fellow at the University of Southampton. He is a Rabbi and is at present Lecturer in Rabbinics at the University of Cambridge. His publications include *Apocrypha: Jewish Literature of the Hellenistic Age* and *Atlas of the Jewish World*, and he has translated a number of books from Hebrew, among them *Elsewhere, Perhaps* by Amos Oz published by Penguin.

THE PSALMS

TRANSLATED BY PETER LEVI

with an introduction by Nicholas de Lange

PENGUIN BOOKS

Penguin Books Ltd, Harmondsworth, Middlesex, England
Viking Penguin Inc., 40 West 23rd Street, New York, New York 10010, U.S.A.
Penguin Books Australia Ltd, Ringwood, Victoria, Australia
Penguin Books Canada Ltd, 2801 John Street, Markham, Ontario, Canada
L3R 1B4
Penguin Books (N.Z.) Ltd, 182–190 Wairau Road, Auckland 10, New Zealand

—

This translation first published 1976
Reprinted 1985

—

Copyright © Peter Levi 1976
Introduction copyright © Nicholas de Lange, 1976
All rights reserved

—

Made and printed in Great Britain by
Cox & Wyman Ltd, Reading
Set in Monotype Bembo

TO THE MEMORY OF
EDUARD FRAENKEL

CONTENTS

TRANSLATOR'S PREFACE

THE Psalms of David are a collection of Hebrew poems or canticles, some of them for use in the Temple at Jerusalem, others for a variety of special purposes. One is apparently for a king's birthday, some refer to pilgrimage, one at least seems to come from the Babylonian exile. They differ widely in date and origin; certain psalms have over-tones of Marduk and of Baal, whose poetry was plundered or adapted for Jewish use. The same phrases are repeated in different psalms with a slightly different emphasis. Very similar poetry, though not on the same rich scale, can be found elsewhere in the Middle East, and the Jewish psalms themselves often show traces of reworking. The unity of the psalms as a collection is simply their basis in Jewish history and worship and now also in Christian tradition.

The question, what kind of poetry they are, is easier to ask than to answer. They are full of word-play, puns and synonyms; verses generally go in couples with the same rhythms and the same syntax, otherwise the metre is free but strong. Some psalms begin consecutive verses with all the letters of the Hebrew alphabet, but this device appears to be decadent; it is certainly no earlier than the introduction of writing. Only the most elaborate of the psalms, 119, is so compli-cated in its form as to be pedantic; it is significant that this psalm is largely concerned with the study of the Law, and seems to have been composed by a student. But the language and form of most of the psalms, and some of their music, seem to be popular, though we are speaking of an age in which court and Temple poetry would not differ greatly from what was sung by herdsmen in the desert. The sudden twists of meaning and feeling, and the uneven and unpredict-able progression of certain psalms, can be traced to such a popular origin. Above all, the morality of the psalms is popular. Their God is the God of natural justice.

Justice is natural and absolute and universal, and God could be seen as a projection of this justice. He is as single as the sky. Some of the earliest psalms are the outcry of a desert people; they are nomadic herdsmen hungry for justice and angry with the various abominations of more settled and civilized peoples. Their monotheism is not unlike that of the Mongols and the early Arabs. But the great mass of the psalms suggest a settled, agricultural society. Psalm 65, for example, is a harvest psalm, and the Temple and pilgrimage psalms glorify the city of Jerusalem. A number of psalms which seem to be individual may be parables of the whole people, but they are clearly based on very personal poetry and some personal psalms certainly exist. The hunger for justice in these psalms is as personal as the continual insistence on honesty and uprightness. In all the psalms God is active and individual, honour is important to him, he is often angry, he can always be relied on but never predicted, he is perfectly straight, he avenges injustice terribly.

It is reasonable to assume that the earliest surviving elements and passages in the psalms have survived in a reworked form, and that the period of exile was formative, in this as in other matters. But the God of the psalms is not only the God of the Law, he is also the personal God of the inward as well as the outward history of the Jews. A living sense of the justice of God survived; it was transmitted as fully by the psalms as by the prophets. This is why the psalms were so important at a later date in the reformative movement in Europe. They were sung in medieval monasteries in Latin and to grave musical settings, and interpreted much in the spirit of the Jewish Midrashic commentaries: what came alive in them at the Reformation was the passionate reliance of the troubled and persecuted on the justice of God. The music they were sung to in Reformation Europe was strong and appropriate, but quite different from the monastic chants. It was no longer a supple musing but a four-square affirmation. It is interesting in this connection that the psalms of the liturgy in the Church of England, that is the Prayer Book psalms, belong to the early years of the Reformation. They were translated by Coverdale in the 1530s and no later version has ever driven them out, not even the Authorized Version, which is largely based on them.

A modern learned commentary on the psalms would be a long book and would take many years to write; a full study of their history and influence would have to be at least equally long. This is a bare translation. I have followed the traditional Hebrew text, usually, though not for the first few psalms, that of the Stuttgart Bible (1969). I have also used the old Latin versions, the new Latin translation commissioned by Pope Pius XII, the Midrash, the Septuagint Greek, the International Critical Commentary (1906) and a number of existing translations. Of these I found Luther helpful and Martin Buber's version wonderful. Many times when I was in doubt Martin Buber confirmed the suspicion that the obvious meaning of the existing text makes better and stronger sense than a far-fetched interpretation or a conjecture. There are some passages in the psalms which do defy interpretation; in a classical text they would be obelized, but I have obelized nothing. I made one conjectural emendation involving a change of one letter. I should make it clear that I knew just enough Hebrew to make this translation using every available aid; I am in no sense a Hebrew scholar.

Of the English versions I got help from Coverdale, the Authorized and the Geneva versions and the Douai Bible, and a little from Knox's version and the New English Bible. I have tried not to substitute without necessity new English phrases for what is old and well-loved, but unity and modernity of language, as well as the true meaning of the Hebrew, have often made changes inevitable. I thought my first duty was to Hebrew, my second to the English language. I have tried to use only the words and phrases of passionate common speech. I was committed from the beginning, not by personal taste but because I believe the language has altered, to doing without 'thou' and 'thee'. For similar reasons I abolished 'the Lord' but felt unwilling to call God 'Yahweh'; I know no one who actually prays to him in English by that name. I therefore translated all the words for God simply as God. The names and titles of God generate many difficulties of translation, and more in the psalms than elsewhere.

On and off, the translation took three years. I would like to record my gratitude to friends for encouragement and help of many kinds during that time, to Mr and Mrs Leigh-Fermor in whose house I started the translation, to Iain and Miranda Watson who lent me a quiet place to continue it, to Mr Anthony O'Hear for pleasant company, to Father Gerry Diamond for ceaseless and thorough advice over my many textual and linguistic difficulties, to my cousin Caryl

Brahms, to Mr Brendan McLaughlin and to Father Paul Hughes for their patience and advice and to Father Ian Brayley for looking through the complete typescript. I am grateful to Nicholas de Lange for much tactful encouragement and friendship. Above all, I must thank Mr Nikos Stavroulakis for his woodcut of King David, with which I have lived until it is part of my mind, and for the long loan of his copy of *The Midrash on Psalms*. And as always I am very genuinely grateful to the members of Campion Hall and to my superiors for their encouragement and their restraint.

PETER LEVI

INTRODUCTION

THE Book of Psalms is an ancient anthology of even more ancient Hebrew songs and poems. The Hebrew Bible preserves a considerablef corpus of ancient poetry, of which the psalms represent only a small fraction. The biblical works were composed over a long perio d o time, and their authorship is for the most part unknown. Their themes cover every aspect of life: victory in war and lament over the fallen, philosophical speculation and folk wisdom, public worship and private prayer, political propaganda and prophecy, sacred and profane love. It is evident that a love of music and poetry was deeply rooted in the people of Israel from its earliest history, and some of the poetry reaches great heights of sensitivity and refinement.

The psalms are mainly religious poems, hymns and prayers and songs of praise to God. Though little is known of their history, it is probable that they once formed part of the public worship of Israel. Some of them are very ancient, dating back beyond 1,000 BC; others are much later. The main period of composition is thought to have been the time of the Davidic monarchy, from about 1,000 BC to its collapse in 586 BC. Ancient tradition makes King David the founder of the worship and the author of many of the psalms. He is described as a skilful lyre-player (1 Samuel 16:15 f.), and several of his poems are quoted in the Bible, for instance his famous laments over Saul and Jonathan (2 Samuel 1:17 ff.) and Abner (ibid., 3:33 f.), and his 'Last Words' (ibid., 23:1 ff.).

There is no way of knowing which, if any, of our psalms were composed by King David, or by his son and successor Solomon (d. *c* 933 BC), who is described (1 Kings 4:32) as the author of one thousand and five poems. The work of composing and performing the psalms was probably in the hands of the special guilds of Temple musicians, who are said to have been first set up and trained by David (1 Chronicles 16:4 ff.). It will have been their task to preserve and add to the corpus of ancient hymns and to rehearse and perform them, and it is perhaps to them that we owe the collection which has come down to us as the Book of Psalms or Psalter.

Not all the psalms which have come down to us are found in the Psalter. Much of the Hebrew Bible, as has already been said, consists of poetry. In the older English translations this was not always apparent, but modern translations generally set out the poetical passages in verse form, and it can consequently be seen at a glance that not only are whole books written in poetry, but most of the other books contain incidental passages in verse, and to some of these we can hardly deny the name of psalms. This impression is fortified by the fact that one psalm, no. 18, reappears in the Second Book of Samuel (Ch. 22), where it is attributed to King David. Some other 'psalms' outside the Psalter are the poem attributed to King Hezekiah (late eighth century BC) (Isaiah 38:10–20), the 'last words of David' (2 Samuel 23), the 'prayer of Hannah' (1 Samuel 2), the 'prayer of Jonah' (Jonah 2), and the 'prayer of Habakkuk' (Habakkuk 3). There is no point in speculating on why these psalms were left out of the Psalter; it is obvious, though, that the ancient editors or compilers of the Psalter were not trying to produce a complete and definitive collection of the Hebrew psalms.

If we cast our net even wider, we can find other ancient Hebrew psalms which were not even included in the Bible, although a few of them found their way into the ancient translations of the Bible and even of the Psalter itself. One example is the poem of thanksgiving in the last chapter of the Book of Ben Sira or Ecclesiasticus (51:1–12), and there are several more in the other 'Apocrypha', the parts of the Greek Bible which were not incorporated in the Hebrew Bible. The Greek translation of the Psalter actually contains one psalm, and the Syriac translation five psalms, which are not found in the Hebrew Psalter.

Our knowledge of the history of the Psalter has been tantalizingly extended by the discoveries of manuscripts in the Judean Desert, the so-called Dead Sea Scrolls, among which are our oldest Hebrew manuscripts of psalms. The importance of these documents is inestimable, since they date back to a period before the Hebrew Bible was edited in its present form. The medieval biblical manuscripts present hardly any variations, and do not differ to any great extent from the printed Hebrew Bibles, but the manuscripts from the Judean Desert do offer us all sorts of important variants, and at the same time they present us with works which were previously completely unknown. In the second category are a number of new psalms, which seem to have been the product of the peculiar sectarian milieu in which the manuscripts were copied and preserved. But there are also several manuscripts which, while they consist mainly of canonical psalms, also contain pieces which are not found in the biblical Psalter as it has come down to us. The most spectacular of these texts includes, interspersed among the biblical psalms, the 'last words of David' (2 Samuel 23), a poem from the end of Ben Sira, three of the psalms which were previously only known indirectly from the ancient translations, and three psalms which were completely unknown before the discovery of this scroll.

All these new discoveries raise fascinating questions about the history of the Psalter, questions which have not yet been properly answered. It is not easy to disentangle how much in the Dead Sea Scrolls is purely sectarian and how much is evidence of the state of the Psalter before it was edited in the form in which it has been handed down to us in the Bible. The only comparative material we have comes from the ancient translations. In these the arrangement of the psalms broadly follows the pattern of the later Hebrew manuscripts, although they include some psalms not found in the Hebrew, while in several of the Dead Sea Scrolls the order of the psalms is quite different.

There does not seem to be any logical principle guiding the arrangement of the psalms within the Psalter. Even the ancient Jewish and Christian commentators, who liked to be able to explain everything in the Bible, were at a loss to explain the order of the psalms. It is not chronological, nor is it thematic. On the other hand it does not seem to be entirely haphazard, since there do seem to be certain groups of psalms which share common features (for example the last five all begin and end with the word *hallelujah*, 'praise God'). Probably the collection we have is based on earlier collections, and parts of it may represent complete smaller collections. (This may explain why some of the psalms occur twice: no. 14, for instance, reappears as no. 53, and part of no. 40 is similar to no. 70.) The present Psalter is divided into five books (Book 1: 1–41; Book 2: 42–72; Book 3: 73–89; Book 4: 90–106; Book 5: 107–150). The divisions are marked by a formula of benediction followed by 'amen' or 'amen and amen', and after the second book the words, 'Here end the prayers of David son of Jesse', are inserted in the Hebrew. The division into books goes back to the ancient editors, and may be intended to reflect the fivefold division of the Books of Moses, the Torah.

The date at which the present collection was made is unknown. It must be later than the latest psalms, of course, but scholars are unable to agree as to which psalms are the latest or when they were composed. Equally it must be earlier than the translation of the Psalter into Greek, which agrees with it substantially apart from some minor variations. The date of this translation is not known precisely, but it was probably made in the course of the second century B C. The Dead Sea texts presenting a different arrangement may also date from the second century or a little later; they may preserve an earlier tradition, or a purely local or sectarian variant, but it is not unreasonable to claim them as evidence that the arrangement of the psalms, at least in parts of the Psalter, was still not quite fixed at this date. Many of the Dead Sea texts, however, agree closely with the Greek Psalter and the later Hebrew manuscript tradition.

In the traditional arrangement of books in the Hebrew Bible the psalms stand first in the third and last division, the Writings. This was the last section of the Bible to be canonized, and contains works not included in the earlier collections of the Torah and Prophets. The canonization of the writings probably took place in the course of the first Christian century, but despite heated disputes about some works there does not seem to have been any argument about the scriptural status of the psalms. Thus Jesus (Luke 24:44) refers to 'the Law of Moses (Torah), the Prophets and the Psalms', and Josephus describes the third division as containing 'psalms to God and precepts for the conduct of human life' (*Against Apion*, 1, 40). The popularity of the psalms is attested by the many manuscript remains (some thirty) from the Dead Sea community, and by frequent quotations in the New Testament and other Jewish writings from the first century and later.

The Dead Sea Scrolls have also provided some fragments of commentaries on psalms, which mark the first step towards the rich later exegetical literature. Many of the Church Fathers wrote commentaries on the psalms, and the rabbinic writings preserve numerous explanations and interpretations by the ancient Rabbis. At some time in the Middle Ages the old rabbinic traditions were collected together in the long Hebrew and Aramaic work known as *The Midrash on Psalms* or *The Seeker of Good* (*Shoher Tov*, an allusion to Proverbs 11:27).

There are traces of early comments in the Psalter itself. Most of the psalms, as they have come down to us in the Hebrew Bible, are provided with headings of various kinds. Some of them refer apparently to the type of composition and the musical rendering; some contain the name of a person (such as David, Solomon, or the Levitical poet Asaph) who is perhaps supposed to be the author; and some of the headings attempt to place the psalms in a historical setting, generally an incident in the life of David. The origin of these headings is not known, and their interpretation is problematical. The technical terms are obscure and mostly defy translation, and the references to personalities and events probably have no historical worth (we may compare the process by which the psalms elsewhere in the Bible were fitted into a vaguely appropriate historical background). It is not even certain that the names in the headings are meant to be those of the authors; the heading usually translated 'of David', for instance, may mean 'for David', 'about David', or even 'part of David's collection'. Moreover, the headings in the Greek Psalter frequently differ from those in the Hebrew – in fact some of the psalms have headings in the Greek but none at all in the Hebrew. The headings are later than the psalms themselves, and presumably represent notes by the collectors and editors about their liturgical use and the (rather fancifully) supposed circumstances of their original composition. In the older English translations it was the practice to include them as if they were part of the psalms themselves; in modern translations the tendency is to leave them out.

The musical headings are a useful reminder, however, that the psalms were performed, like most ancient poetry, to musical accompaniment. Although the music is unfortunately lost, we know the names of some of the instruments and different forms of musical presentation, since they are mentioned in the psalms themselves and elsewhere in the Bible. The word 'psalm' comes from a Greek word meaning originally the music of a stringed instrument. The Hebrew headings contain various technical terms for different kinds of songs; eventually a single generic term came into use, *Tehillim*, which means 'songs of praise' (from the same root as *Hallel*), and reflects both the character of the poems and their use in the Temple and later in the Synagogue. Although probably not all the psalms were originally written for public worship, in time they were absorbed into the cult, and were performed by professional groups of trained musicians. Many of them refer explicitly to the function of music in the singing of God's praise (e.g. nos. 33, 92, 150).

Scholars have been at great pains to analyse the psalms and arrange them into various types. They have distinguished psalms of the individual and of the community, hymns, laments and thanksgivings, songs of pilgrimage and songs of wisdom, and also a class of 'royal psalms' which either celebrate the king (e.g. nos. 2, 45, 110) or express the king's thoughts on his relations with God and with his people. Interesting though this kind of analysis is, it does not bring us closer to an appreciation of the poems, and indeed many of them defy categorization. What strikes the reader far more than the similarity of types is the imagery of the psalms, and the personal and national situations they depict. We frequently find the poets musing on the contrast between good and evil, which is the theme of the first psalm in the book (which was perhaps intended by the compilers as an introduction to the whole work). Life is full of dangers, both natural and man-made; the life of the individual and the nation is precarious, and constantly threatened by hostile forces, enmity, malice and death. In contrast, God's saving power is ever-sure, and a life of virtue and trust in God can overcome envy, menace and distress.

The psalms present us with a distillation of the biblical belief in God as the guardian of his people (no. 121) and the champion of the poor and needy (no. 113); who demands justice and sits in judgement, and deals out rewards and punishments. All these aspects of his activity are closely connected, and the poets take it for granted that the connection is obvious. In no. 68, for instance, the words 'father of the fatherless, justice of widowed women . . .' are followed by a description of God marching through the desert at the head of his people. A characteristic of many of the psalms is that they retell the history of the people. In one case (no. 136) the history begins with the creation of the world, and there are several allusions to the covenant with Abraham, Isaac and Jacob (e.g. no. 105), but the commonest historical reference is to the Exodus from Egypt: the plagues, the miraculous crossing of the Red Sea and the journey through the wilderness to the promised land (nos. 106, 114, 135). These psalms may have originated in the liturgy for the Passover festival. The story is told as a proud and joyful testimonial to God's power and faithfulness, but it also contains an exhortation to right behaviour, and a plea to God to continue his saving activity. No. 116 presents all these elements: beginning with a shout of praise, *Hallelujah!* (Praise God!), it continues with a commendation to justice and right action, and then goes on, rather surprisingly, to list in detail the sins of the people, who abandoned and disobeyed God at every point in the history of the Exodus. The psalm ends with a reaffirmation of God's faithfulness, and a prayer for help which is linked again to God's praise, the closing word being again *Hallelujah!*

No. 78 has a similar theme, though the poet presents it in a different and less straightforward form. He tells how the people repeatedly forgot God's wonderful actions on their behalf, beginning with the very generation which came out of Egypt, and continuing after the settlement in the promised land. Each time the people forget the wonders and rebel against God, and each time he punishes them. Eventually he rejects the tribe of Ephraim, son of Joseph, and chooses instead the tribe of Judah, in the person of David; he allows his holy residence at Shiloh to be destroyed and takes up residence instead on Mount Zion, in the Hills of Judah.

The idea of Mount Zion as God's place of residence recurs again and again in the psalms, and serves as a reminder of their origin in the worship of God in the Temple at Jerusalem. Jerusalem was a centre of pilgrimage, and many of the psalms are specifically connected with the great pilgrim festivals. Psalms 120–134 all carry the heading 'A Pilgrim Song', and it is here that we feel particularly vividly the devotion of the pilgrim, but there are references to Zion and Jerusalem throughout the Psalter, and if we want to understand the psalms in their historical setting it is on the worship of the Temple that we must focus our attention. It was this worship which played the central role in the national and religious life of the people of Israel, giving concrete and visible expression to the idea of the special relationship between God and his people. The psalms convey vividly the feeling that God protects his people as 'the mountains stand around Jerusalem' (no. 125). His saving power and faithfulness are a matter of everyday experience, in the life of the individual and of the community. The references to history, though they are occasionally to clearly identifiable historical events, frequently interpret history in a *typical* sense, that is they take up certain historical situations and regard them as general historical models. No. 74, for instance, speaks of the destruction of the Temple. We cannot know whether this was the Babylonian destruction of 587 BC, or the desecration of the Temple by Antiochus Epiphanes in 186 BC, or some other unknown event. It hardly matters: what we have is a typical situation – the destruction of the Temple (which is also the theme of certain Babylonian and Canaanite laments) – interpreted in a religious sense. Again, no. 83 presents a list of enemies who have joined together (cf. no. 2) to destroy Israel. Once more, we are unable to identify any particular historical occasion, and indeed it is unlikely that all these enemies ever existed at the same time: they may simply represent a typical occurrence, the threatening of Jerusalem, which lay at a crossroads of the Near East, by an enemy. The threat is countered by an equally typical list of God's victories over other armies who had threatened his people.

In view of the close connection between the psalms and the worship in the Temple, which was based on sacrifices, it is remarkable that several of the psalms criticize the sacrifice of animals. No. 50 condemns the attitude that thinks that God desires sacrifices, particularly when this attitude is coupled with the practice or toleration of immorality. Every living creature in the world belongs to God; he has no need of gifts of animals from men. The true sacrifice is 'the sacrifice of thanksgiving' and a life devoted to right action. A similar outlook finds expression in nos. 40 and 51. The condemnation of sacrifices was not universally accepted, however. At a later date a postscript was added to no. 51, which bluntly contradicted the message of the poem.

The idea of the study and observance of God's teachings as the central core of the religion, which was to find its fullest expression after the final destruction of sacrificial worship, is present in several of the psalms, and is developed in great detail in the longest psalm, no. 119, which is an extended eulogy of the 'teachings of the Lord' and a prayer for enlightenment. This psalm is reminiscent of the so-called 'Wisdom Literature', the biblical books of Proverbs, Job and Kohelet (Ecclesiastes), and the Wisdom of Ben Sira (Ecclesiasticus) which is not included in the Bible. The characteristic of these poetical works is the philosophical investigation of the meaning of life, expressed in the form of teachings about right and wrong, happiness and misery, life and death. Several of the psalms belong to this genre (e.g. nos. 1, 49, 112), and the same themes recur frequently elsewhere in the psalms, often linked to the praise of God (e.g. nos. 25, 34, 62). These poems often quote familiar maxims from the wisdom literature: 'The fear of God is the beginning of wisdom', for example, in no. 111, echoes Proverbs 1:7 and 9:10, and Job 28:28.

If there is one common thread running through all the psalms it is the praise of God's lovingkindness, as it is reflected in nature and in the experience both of the individual and of God's people. Whether the dominant note is one of praise or thanksgiving, of terror or distress, of philosophical reflection or of solemn celebration, there is barely a single psalm which does not contain a reference to God's love, his saving power, his faithfulness and loyalty to those who trust in him.

The simple faith of the psalms and the overwhelming sense they convey of God's nearness and power is probably the main reason why their popularity has never worn out, and why they have remained at the heart of the personal and public worship of both Jews and Christians up to the present day. As they survived through many centuries in the service of the Temple in Jerusalem, so they survived the destruction of that Temple by a Roman army in AD 70 and the extinction of the ancient sacrificial cult, and were enthusiastically taken over into the worship of the Jewish Synagogue and the Christian Church. In the Temple, many of the psalms had been performed on specific days in the sacred year (particularly during the great autumn pilgrim-festival). In the Synagogue and the Church, too, certain psalms are particularly connected with special days. Thus for Jews no. 92 is a Sabbath psalm, no. 51 belongs to the Day of Atonement, and the group, nos. 113–118 (the *Hallel*), is recited as a liturgy of praise of God on all the major festivals. The Church, too, selected certain psalms for particular days, and in addition the practice grew up of reciting the complete Psalter in the course of each week or each month. The simple beauty and spiritual appeal of the psalms have assured their place in private as well as communal prayer, and they have remained, over the centuries, the most profound expression of their religious feelings for Jews and Christians alike.

NICHOLAS DE LANGE

A NOTE ON HEBREW POETRY

ANY reader of poetry in translation naturally wonders how much he has lost of the poetic form of the original. In the case of ancient Hebrew poetry the loss is less than in the case of many other languages. Hebrew poetry relies for its effect mainly on elements which are, broadly speaking, translatable. There is relatively little formal structure, and the poetic effect is achieved primarily through the marshalling and deployment of images and ideas.

In Hebrew, verbs and nouns are expanded by the addition of prefixes and suffixes corresponding in English to pronouns, prepositions and conjunctions. In this way, solid blocks of meaning are built up, each with one main stress. There are thus far fewer words in the Hebrew than in the English translation, and none of the long strings of monosyllables which are common in English.

Because of the grammatical structure of the words there is often a rhyme, but it is almost accidental, and hardly seems to be exploited by the poets. They do, however, make very effective use of rhythm and of assonance. A more obviously artificial device is the acrostic, where successive lines or groups of lines begin with successive letters of the alphabet. This occurs in several psalms, the most elaborate being no. 119, which consists of stanzas of eight lines beginning with each of the twenty-two letters of the Hebrew alphabet.

For the most part, however, Hebrew poetry does not observe the familiar English structure of regular lines and verses. The words are arranged into units of sense, frequently consisting of only two or three words. These units are further arranged in groups of two or three, and these groups may in turn be arranged in larger groups. There is nothing regular or consistent about the arrangement, and it is not always easy to analyse. The flexibility of the poetic form is one of the strengths of Hebrew poetry, and it is often exploited to produce striking effects.

The principal formal feature of the poetry, then, for all its intangibility, is the balance between the units. The balance is achieved not just through the arrangements of words and stressed syllables, but through the arrangement of ideas. Here, too, there is great flexibility, and there are no discernible rules, but the effect is undeniable.

In any pair of units the second may echo the first in one of several ways, or it may complement or expand it. It may express the same idea in different words, or a different idea in similar words. It may repeat a word, or replace it by a synonym or antonym. It may contain a different form of the same word, or the same form of a different word. The order of the words may be altered, or even reversed. The second unit may be longer or shorter than the first. Sometimes a part of the first unit may be abandoned, or replaced by something quite different. And often the two units together lead on to a third, which takes up their idea and expands it yet further, or serves as a conclusion.

All this may best be illustrated by some examples taken from the psalms, with a simplified transliteration of the Hebrew and an approximate word-by-word translation:

vadonaí		*le ʻolám*	*yeshév*
and-God		for-ever	sits
	konén	*lamishpát*	*kisó*
	setting-up	for-judgement	his-throne
vehú	*yishpót*	*tevél*	*betsédek*
and-he	judges	the-world	with-justice
	yadín	*leumím*	*bemeisharím*
	judges	peoples	with-justice
vihí	*adonaí*	*misgáv*	*ladákh*
and-be	God	a-stronghold	for-the-oppressed
	misgáv	*le ʻitót*	*batsaráh*
	a-stronghold	for-times	in-trouble
			(Psalm 9)

| *hashamáim* | | *mesaperím* | *kevod-él* |
| the-heavens | | telling | God's-glory |

uma 'aséh
and-the-work

yadáv
of-his-hands

magíd
telling

harakía'
the-sky

yóm
day

leyóm
to-day

yabía'
pours-out

ómer
speech

velaílah
and-night

lelaílah
to-night

yehaveh-dá'at
tells-knowledge
    (Psalm 19)

esá
I-raise

'einaí
my-eyes

el-heharím
to-the-mountains

meáyin
whence

yavó
comes

'ezrí
my-help

'ezrí
my-help

meím
from

adonaí
God

'oséh
making

shamáim
heaven

vaárets
and-earth

al-yitén
let-him-not-let

lamót
stumble

reglékha
your-foot

al-yanúm
let-him-not-be-
drowsy

shomrékha
guarding-you

hinéh
indeed

lo-yanúm
he-will-not-be-
drowsy

veló
and-not

yishán
sleep

shomér
guarding

yisraél
Israel

adonaí
God

shomrékha
guarding-you

adonaí	*tsilkhá*	*'al-yád*	*yeminékha*
God	your-shadow	on-the-hand	your-right
yomám	*hashémesh*	*lo-yakéka*	
by-day	the-sun	will-not-strike-you	
veyaréah	*balaílah*		
and-moon	in-the-night		
adonaí	*yishmorkhá*	*mikol-rá'*	
God	will-guard-you	from-all-evil	
	yishmór	*et-nafshékha*	
	will-guard	your-soul	
adonaí	*yishmor-tsetkhá*	*uvoékha*	
God	will-guard-your-leaving	and-your-arriving	
me 'atáh	*ve 'ad- 'olám*		
from-now	and-for-ever		

(Psalm 121)

SUGGESTIONS
FOR FURTHER READING

GENERAL INTRODUCTION AND COMMENTARY:

C. F. Barth, *Introduction to the Psalms*, Blackwell, Oxford, 1966.

J. H. Eaton, *Psalms: Introduction and Commentary*, SCM Press, 1967.

S. Mowinckel, *The Psalms in Israel's Worship*, Blackwell, Oxford, 1962.

A. B. Rhodes, *The Psalms*, SCM Press, 1961.

H. Ringgren, *The Faith of the Psalmists*, SCM Press, 1963.

S. Terrien, *The Psalms and their Meaning for Today*, Bobs-Merrill, Indianapolis, Ind., 1952.

A. Weiser, *The Psalms: A Commentary*, SCM Press, 1962.

DEAD SEA SCROLLS:

S. Holm-Nielsen, *Hodayot: Psalms from Qumran*, Universitetsforlaget i Aarhus, 1960.

J. A. Sanders, *The Dead Sea Psalms Scroll*, Cornell University Press, Ithaca, N.Y., 1967.

G. Vermes, *The Dead Sea Scrolls in English*, Penguin, 1962.

THE MIDRASH:

The Midrash on Psalms, translated by W. G. Braude, Yale University Press, New Haven, Conn., 1959.

THE PSALMS

I

O blessings of that man
who has not paced about among the wicked
or stood in a sinful road
or sat down among mockers.
Night and day he meditates the law of God.
He is like a tree planted beside a stream of water,
which will be full of fruit in summer
and its leaves will not shrivel up:
his work will be prosperous.
That is not true of the wicked:
they are like the chaff of grain, the wind carries them away.
The wicked will not survive in the judgement
nor the sinners in the gathering of the just.
Because God knows the road of the just,
and the road of the wicked will die out.

Why are the nations of the world unquiet
and the people full of fantasies?
The kings of the earth and all the rulers have stood up
    together,
against God and against his anointed one.
Break off the chains, we shall throw away the ropes.
He is laughing in heaven: God will make a joke of them.
He will speak angrily, he will handle them with fury.
I have planted my king on Zion, which is my holy moun-
    tain.
I declare this law:
God said to me, you are my son, I have given birth to you
    today.
Ask me and I will give you the nations of the world for an
    inheritance
and the ends of the earth for an estate.
You will break them to pieces with an iron rod,
you will shatter them like pottery.
Kings, be wise; judges of the earth, be warned:
Be afraid and serve God,
tremble and be glad.
Kiss the son,
for fear he might be angry and you might be destroyed:
his anger blazes up quickly.
Happy is the man who shelters with him.

3

O God, how many enemies I have now.
Many rise up against me,
many speak about my life,
saying there is no hope for me in God.
God, you are my shield, my glory, you lift up my head.
I shall cry out to God with my voice,
and God will answer out of his holy mountain.
I lay down and I fell asleep,
I have woken because God has hold of me.
I shall not fear thousands all around me.
Rise up God, save me my God.
You have struck the bones of all the faces of my enemies,
you have broken the teeth of the wicked.
God saves. God blesses his people.

4

God of justice, answer me when I cry out.
You let me loose from troubles;
be gracious, hear my prayer.
Children of men, how long shall I be honoured with dis-
    honour?
How long will you love nothingness and lies?
Know this: God has singled out his holy one,
God will hear me when I cry out.
Tremble and do no wickedness,
speak in your heart on your bed and be silent.
Give the sacrifice of justice and trust God.
Many ask, Who will make us see good things?
God, lift up the light of your face on us.
You have given my heart gladness in more abundance than
    the season with the crops and the fresh wine.
I shall lie down in peace to sleep;
O God, you alone will make me live in safety.

God, listen to my words,
consider my meditations,
hear me when I cry out, king and God.
I shall pray, God, and you will hear my voice;
I shall speak to you and wait for you in the early morning.
Because you are not a god delighting in wickedness,
and an evil man cannot live beside you.
The boasters cannot stand up in your sight.
You hate all doers of wickedness.
You will destroy speakers against the truth,
God shall hate the man of blood and of deceit.
And I shall go into your house in the abundance of your
   goodness,
I shall bow to the temple of your holiness and I shall fear
   you.
God of justice, guide me, because of my enemies;
make your path straight for me.
There is no faithfulness in their mouth,
and their inner parts are destruction;
their throat is an open grave,
and all their tongues are smooth.
God, put the guilt on them,
they shall fall by their devices.
Drive them away because of the great quantity of their
   crimes,
because they have revolted against you.

6

O God, do not rebuke me with anger, do not punish me
with fury.

O God, be good to me, because I am sick;

O God, heal me, because my bones shake.

My soul is very troubled. O God, how long?

O God, return, and save my soul, because you are merciful.

Because in death there is no remembrance of you, who will
thank you in hell?

I have groaned until I was tired,

I shall wash my sheets with my tears night after night,

I shall melt my bed with my tears.

My eyes have wasted with sorrow, they have grown old
because of my enemies.

Go away from me, doers of wickedness, because God has
listened to the voice of my weeping.

God has heard me when I cried to him, God will receive
my prayer.

My enemies shall be ashamed and greatly troubled;

they shall suddenly turn away and be ashamed.

7

God, God, my refuge, rescue me from my persecuters;
save me before they tear out my soul and pull it to pieces
    like lions
and there is no one to save me.
God, God, if I am guilty, if there is evil on my hands,
if I did wrong to my friend, and yet I saved my enemy who
    was so without reason,
let my enemy hunt my soul, let him take it,
let him trample my life into the earth,
let him put down my honour in the dust.
Rise up, God, be angry, rise up against the raging of my
    enemies.
Wake because of me: you have commanded judgement.
The gathering of peoples shall be around you; rise and
    stand over them.
God will judge the peoples; judge me, God, for my justice
    and the innocence that is in me.
Let the wicked man's crimes have an end,
strengthen the just man.
God looks into the heart and the bowels, and he is just.
God is my shield, he saved the true heart;
God judges with justice, God is angry every day.
If a man will not turn back, God sharpens his sword;
he has bent his bow, he has aimed it.
He has prepared the instruments of death for that man,
he will make his arrows burning.
The man conceives wickedness, he is pregnant with harm,
    he gives birth to deceit;
he has dug a pit, and deepened it;
now he has fallen into the pit he dug.

9

The harm will come on his own head,
his violence will come down on the crown of his head.
I shall thank God for his justice,
I shall sing songs to the name of the most high God.

O God our lord, how great your name is over all the earth.

Through this you have set up your greatness above the
heavens.

You have put power into the mouths of children and of
babies, against your enemies,

to silence the enemy and the avenger.

When I see the heavens, the work of your fingers,

and the sun and the moon which you have built,

what is man, that you should remember him?

what is the son of Adam, that you should trouble over him?

Yet you made him only a little less than a god,

you have crowned his head with glory and honour.

You have made him govern the works of your hands,

you have put everything under his feet,

sheep and cattle and the animals of the country,

the birds in heaven and the fish in the sea that travel on the
pathways of the seas.

O God our lord, how excellent your name is over all the
earth.

9

I will thank God with my whole heart,
I will speak about all your wonderful work.
I will rejoice and be glad over you,
I will sing songs to your name, O most high.
My enemies shall be turned back and stumble and be des-
    troyed because of your presence,
because you have maintained my right and my argument,
you sat on your throne and gave judgement and it was just.
You have rebuked peoples and destroyed wicked men,
you have blotted out their name for ever.
They are utterly consumed into ruins,
you have plucked up their cities and the memory of them
    has passed away.
God shall sit for ever, he has fixed his throne of law;
he shall judge the world with justice, and give true judge-
    ment to the peoples.
And God shall be a high castle for the oppressed,
a castle in times of destitution.
And those who know your name shall have confidence in
    you,
because you have not abandoned those who look for you,
    O God.
Sing songs to God who lives in Zion,
tell his deeds among the peoples.
Because he remembered and demanded blood,
and did not forget the crying out of the afflicted.
God, be good to me, see how I am afflicted by persecuters,
you lift me from the doors of death:
so that I may praise you in the doors of the daughters of
    Zion,

and be glad that you can save.

The peoples have fallen down into the pit they dug,
their foot was caught in the net they hid.

God is known, he has given his judgement,
the wicked man is caught in the snare he made with his own
hands.

The wicked shall go down to hell – everyone who forgets
God.

The poor will not be forgotten for ever,
nor shall their expectation be wasted for ever.

Rise up, God, do not let man strengthen himself;
when you come the peoples will be judged.

O God, put fear into them, let the peoples know that they
are men.

O God, why do you stand at a distance?
Why do you hide in the seasons of distress?
The wicked man is very proud and persecutes the poor,
and the poor man is trapped in his schemes.
The wicked man has boasted with the lust of his soul;
he has given up God, he has despised God.
With the pride of his eyes, he will not look for God,
all his thoughts say there is no God.
His road will always be safe; your judgement will fly above
    his head;
he will blow at his enemies with a puff of breath.
He has said in his heart, I shall not be overturned,
and for generation after generation I shall not suffer.
His mouth is full of curses and deceit and persecution,
he has wickedness and wrong under his tongue.
He sits in ambush in the villages
and kills the innocent in quiet places.
His eye watches against the poor man,
and he prepares his ambush in a quiet place,
like a lion in cover.
He ambushes the poor man, he catches him and pulls him
    down in a net.
The unhappy man is crushed, he falls, he is taken by great
    strength.
He has said in his heart, God has forgotten, he has hidden
    his face for ever,
God sees nothing.
O God, rise up; O God, lift your hand and remember the
    poor.
Why has the wicked man despised God?

He has said in his heart, God demands nothing.
And you see this: you are attentive to wrong and suffering,
you take them in your hand;
the poor are left to you, you help the fatherless.
Break the arm of the wicked and the evil man:
you will seek out his wickedness until there is nothing.
God is king for ever and ever,
the nations have died out in his country.
O God, you heard the wishes of the humble,
you have fixed their hearts, and your ears listen,
to be the judge of the fatherless and the persecuted,
so that man on the earth shall not terrorize any more.

God is my refuge.

So how do you say to my soul, Fly away to your hilltop
like a bird?

Because the wicked bend their bows, their arrows are ready
on the string

to shoot down the innocent-hearted in darkness.

When the foundations of the world give way, what can a
just man do?

God is in the temple of his holiness, God has his throne in
the heavens.

His eyes will see and his look will test the sons of Adam.

God shall test the just man,

but his soul hates the wicked man and the lover of violence.

He shall rain down fire and molten rock on the wicked,

their drinking cup will be a burning wind,

because God is just and loves justice,

and the innocent, honest man will see his face.

Save, O God, because the holy are finished,
and there are no more faithful among the sons of Adam.
A man tells lies to his neighbour with a smooth mouth
and with two thoughts in his heart.
God will cut away the smooth mouths and the inflated
  words:
they said, We shall win with words,
we have our mouth and who is our master?
And God will say, Now I shall rise up
because of the persecution of the poor and the groaning of
  the destitute.
I shall make them safe because they sigh to be safe.
The words of God are pure words,
like silver melted down in a furnace of baked earth and
  refined seven times.
O God, you will guard them, and preserve them from this
  generation for ever.
The wicked shall walk round and round;
the worthless ones among the sons of Adam shall be lifted
  up.

O God, how long? Will you forget me for ever?
How long will you hide your face from me?
How long shall I think thoughts in my soul
and have sorrow in my heart all day?
How long will my enemy be lifted above me?
God, O God, see me and answer me;
brighten my eyes
or I shall die and sleep,
and my enemy will say, I have overcome him;
and those that trouble me will be glad, because I was taken
    away.
I have trusted your goodness, let my heart be saved and be
    glad.
I will sing a song to God, because he has rewarded me.

The fool has said in his heart, There is no God.

They are corrupt, they have done abominable things, no one does good.

God looked down from heaven at the sons of Adam

to see if there was anyone who understood and who looked for God.

They have all turned aside and every one of them has become filthy;

and no one does good, not one of them.

Those criminals have eaten my people like they eat bread,

and did they not know?

They have not cried out to God.

They were afraid and very much afraid,

because God is with the just in their generation.

You dishonour the poor man's thoughts, but God is his refuge.

Will he come from Zion to save Israel?

Be glad, Jacob, because God overturns the captivity of his people;

and Israel, be very glad.

15

O God, who shall live in your tent?
Who shall rest on your holy hill?
He who walks innocently, and does rightly,
and speaks the truth in his heart.
There is no slander in his mouth,
he has done no wrong to his neighbour, he has no complaint
    against his neighbour.
He despises the unjust, and he honours those who fear God.
If he swears and his word hurts him he will not call it back.
He has never lent money for profit
nor taken bribes against an honest man.
The man who does all this shall never fall.

Keep me, God my refuge.
I said to God, You are my master, I have no other good.
My delight is the holy ones on earth and the very good.
Those who change their God increase their troubles.
I shall not make the offering to them,
which is blood poured out,
nor will I have their name in my mouth.
God is my share and my right and my cup to drink,
God maintains my right.
My part is in a pleasant place, my inheritance is good.
I shall bless God, who taught me and instructed my body in
    the night.
I have put God in front of me for ever,
God is on my right hand and I shall not fall.
Therefore my heart is glad and my honour is triumphant,
and my flesh shall live safely.
Because you will not leave my soul in hell
or allow your holy one to see the pit.
You will show me and I shall know the path of life,
there is complete gladness in your presence,
your right hand is full of pleasures for ever.

O God hear justice, listen to my cry,
listen to my prayer, there are no lies in my mouth.
My rights shall stand because of your presence,
your eyes shall see uprightness.
You have tried my heart, and come to it in the night;
you have tried me, you will not find anything;
I wanted my words to be just.
In what men do I have kept from the roads of the violent
because of your words.
When I moved I have kept closely in your tracks
and my feet have not slipped.
I called because you will answer me, O God,
listen to me, hear what I say.
Make your mercies wonderful, because your right hand
  saves those that run from their enemies.
Keep me like the apple of your eye,
cover me under the shadow of your wings;
from the wicked that hurt me and my soul's enemies all
  around me.
They have shut up their hearts with fat and they speak
  proudly.
When we move now they are all around us,
they have fixed their eyes to bend us to the ground.
They are like a lion whose pleasure is to tear to pieces,
like a young lion that crouches in quiet places.
Rise up, God, confront him and throw him down, use your
  sword,
set my soul free from the wicked man.
From men, O God, from men who are in the world who
  have their share of life;

you fill their stomachs with your riches, they have sons and
  are satisfied, they leave plenty to their children.
But because of justice I shall see your face,
and I shall wake and see you and be satisfied.

I will love you, O God my strength,
God my crag, my fortress, my rescue.
My God is my rock, I will run to him,
God is my shield and the trumpet of my salvation and my
    castle.
I praise God, I shall cry out to him and be rescued from my
    enemies.
The ropes of death were around me,
I am afraid of the rivers of death.
The strings of hell were around me,
I saw the snare of death.
In my distress I shall cry to God,
he will hear my voice in his temple, and my crying will
    reach him.
The earth quaked and trembled,
and the foundations of the hills shivered and trembled,
    because he was angry.
Smoke came from his nostrils and a devouring fire came out
    of his mouth; it kindled coal.
He bent heaven downwards and descended
and there was darkness under his feet.
He rode on the back of an angel and he flew,
he dropped on the wings of the wind.
He shall make darkness his hiding place and clouds of dark
    water his tent.
Out of his brightness through the deep clouds there came
    hail and blazing coal.
God thundered in heaven, the most high one uttered his
    voice with hail and blazing coal.

He shot his arrows and they were scattered,
he shot his lightning and they were confounded.
The bottom of the sea appeared, and the foundations of the
world were laid open,
because of your furious words, O God,
and because of the blast of your breath.
God will send down and take me, he will lift me out of deep
water.
He will rescue me from my strong enemy and from all
those who hate me,
because they are stronger than I am.
On the day of my disaster I shall meet them face to face,
but God is my support,
he has brought me out into an easy place,
he will rescue me because he is delighted with me.
God will deal with me according to my justice,
he will pay me according to the cleanness of my hands.
Because I have kept to the ways of God;
I have not wickedly gone away from him.
Because all his judgements were in my mind
and I shall not forget any of his laws.
I was honest in the sight of God, I kept myself out of
wickedness.
And God payed me according to my justice
and the cleanness of my hands in his sight.
You will be merciful with the merciful, you will be honest
with an honest man,
and pure with a clean man and dangerous with a hard man,
because you will save a persecuted people
and make arrogant eyes look down.
You will make my light shine,
God who is my God will lighten my darkness.
With your help I shall run through regiments of men,

with the help of God I shall jump over the wall.
God is upright in his ways, the word of God is pure,
he is a shield over everyone who runs to him.
What God is there but God? What rock is there except our
  God?
The God who ties strength on me like a belt
and who makes my path good.
He makes my feet run like a deer,
he puts me to stand on high places.
He has taught my hands war,
so that my arms shall bend back a bow of bronze.
You have given me the shield of salvation,
you will hold me with your right hand,
your carefulness will make me great.
You make me step strongly and my ankles do not totter.
I shall pursue my enemies and overtake them,
I shall not turn back until they are finished.
I shall break them to pieces, they will not be able to rise,
they will fall under my feet.
You have tied strength on me like a belt for war,
you will bring down under me everyone who rises against
  me.
You have given me the backs of my enemies
and I shall wipe out those who have hated me.
They shall cry out and no one will save them,
they shall cry out to God and he will not answer.
I shall grind them to pieces like dust on the face of the wind,
I shall drop them like the mud in the streets.
You shall set me free from the struggles of the people
and make me the head of nations:
a people I never knew shall be under me.
When they hear they shall obey me;
the sons of strangers shall show that they fear me.

The sons of strangers will lose their colour, and tremble
and come out of their fortresses.
God lives, I bless God who is my rock.
I praise God who has saved me:
the God who gives me revenge and puts peoples under me,
who sets me free from my enemies.
Yes, you shall lift me up above those who stand up against
    me
and rescue me from the violent man.
Therefore I will thank you, God among nations,
I will sing songs to your name.
God has saved his king with great actions,
he has done good to his anointed one,
to David and his descendants for ever.

Heaven declares the glory of God,
the sky shows the work of his hands.
Day utters to day,
night shows knowledge to night
without speaking and without language,
and their voice is not heard.
But their sound has gone out to the whole of the earth,
and their words to the ends of the world.
God has made a tent for the sun:
he is like a bridegroom coming out of his tent,
he will delight in running like a strong man.
He goes out from the end of heaven,
and the track where he runs comes to the end of heaven,
and nothing is hidden from the heat of it.
The law of God is perfect, it refreshes the soul.
The witness of God is steady, it makes the simple wise.
The teaching of God is straight, it gladdens the heart;
his command is pure, it enlightens the eyes.
The fear of God is clean, and it stands for ever.
His judgements are the truth, they are all just.
They are more to be desired than gold, more than a great
    quantity of pure gold,
they are sweeter than honey or the dripping of a honey-
    comb.
And your servant is warmed by them,
there is a great reward in observing them.
Who will pick out my sins?
Clean me from secret guilt.
Keep your servant from actions of pride,
do not let pride be my master;

so that I shall be perfect and not guilty of a great sin.
Be pleased with the words in my mouth and the thoughts
 in my heart,
O God my rock and my rescue.

God will answer on the day of distress,
in the name of the God of Jacob you will be lifted up high.
He will send help from his holy place,
he will come from Zion and hold you.
He will remember every offering
and be pleased with the fatness of your burnt offerings.
He will give you the wish of your heart
and make all your thoughts come true.
We shall shout for joy because you have saved us,
we shall fly flags in the name of our God.
May God make all your prayers come true.
Now I know that God has saved his anointed one,
he shall answer him out of his holy heaven,
he saves by the mighty action of his right hand.
Some speak of chariots, others speak of horses,
but we shall speak the name of God who is our God.
They have bowed down and fallen,
and we have risen and stood upright.
God save the king, and answer us on the day that we cry
out.

O God, the king will be glad because of your strength,
he shall rejoice and be very glad because of your salvation.
You have given him the wish of his heart,
you have not refused what he asked for in his words.
You will visit him and bless him with goodness,
and crown his head with a crown of pure gold.
He asked for life, and you gave him a long length of days
for ever and ever.
His glory is great because you have saved him,
you have made him glorious and beautiful.
Because you will bless him for ever
and make him rejoice and be very glad because of your
    presence.
The confidence of the king is in God,
and through the goodness of the most high he shall stand
    and not fall.
Your hand will reach out to all your enemies,
your right hand will reach everyone that has hated you.
You will destroy the fruit of their bodies on the earth,
their posterity among the sons of Adam.
They set out to hurt you and they made their plan,
but they shall not win.
You will make them turn their shoulders,
you will point the strings of your bow against their faces.
Rise up God, be strong;
we will make music and sing about your mightiness.

My God, my God, why have you left me alone?
Salvation is far off from my roaring.
O God, I will cry out in the day and you will not answer,
and at night and I shall not rest.
Holy one, praise of Israel,
our fathers trusted you, they trusted and you saved them.
They cried out to you and they escaped,
they trusted you and they were not shamed.
I am a worm and not a man,
I am a curse-word among men and despised by the people.
When they see me they mock me,
they open their mouths and they wag their heads.
Throw yourself on God: let him rescue him.
Let him save him if he was pleased with him.
You drew me out of the womb of my mother,
you made me trust when I was on her breast.
I was thrust on you from the womb;
from my mother's body you are my God.
Do not be far from me, because distress is close to me
and there is no one to help.
There are wild bulls all around me,
the strong bulls of Bashan are around me.
They have opened their mouth like a lion
to roar and to tear to pieces.
I have been poured out like water,
and all my bones have been separated.
My heart is like wax, it has melted in my bowels.
My strength has dried like baked earth,
my tongue has stuck to the roof of my mouth,
you have put me down in the dust of death.

There are dogs round me,
I am cut off by a crowd of wicked men.
They have torn my hands and my feet,
I can number all my bones.
They will see me and stare.
They will divide my clothes between them:
they will share them out by lot.
O God, do not be far away; O my strength, hurry to help
me.
Save my soul from the sword, and my life from the dog.
Save me from the lion's mouth and the horns of the wild
bulls.
I will tell your name to my brother.
I will praise you in the assembly.
You that fear God, praise him;
and all the blood of Jacob give him glory;
and all the blood of Israel be afraid of God.
Because he did not despise or abominate the poverty of the
poor man;
he heard him when he cried out.
I will praise you in the great assembly,
I will pay my promises in the sight of those that fear God.
The poor shall eat and have enough;
those that have looked for God shall praise him;
may your hearts live for ever.
The ends of the whole earth shall remember and turn to-
wards God,
all the families of nations will bow down to God.
Because God is king, and God is the king of nations.
All those that were strong on the earth have eaten and
bowed down,
and everyone that goes down to the dust whose soul cannot
live shall bow to him.

The descendants will serve him.
They shall speak to the new generation.
They shall tell his justice to a people that will be born:
what God has done.

23

God is my shepherd, I shall not want.
He will bring me into meadows of young grass,
he will guide me beside quiet water.
He will strengthen my soul;
he will lead me in the path of justice, because of his name.
And when I walk in the valley of the darkness of death
I shall fear no evil, because you are with me,
your crook and your staff will be my comfort.
You will set a table for me in front of my enemies;
you have anointed my head with oil, and my cup over-
     flows.
Your goodness and your mercy shall certainly follow me
     through all the days of my life,
and I shall live in the house of God for the length of my
     days.

God possesses the earth and its fullness,
and the whole world and everyone who lives in it.
He built it to stand on the sea,
he founded it on the streams of the rivers.
Who shall climb up to the hill of God?
Who shall stand in his holy place?
The clean-handed and the pure-hearted man.
He has not puffed up his mind with vanity,
nor has he sworn and deceived.
He shall receive the blessing of God,
and the justice of the God of salvation.
That is the generation of those that look for him,
who ask for the face of the God of Jacob.
Lift up your heads, you gates.
Be lifted up, you everlasting gates,
for the king of glory to come in.
Who is this king of glory?
The great and strong God, God who is strong in battle.
Lift up your heads, you gates.
Be lifted up, you everlasting gates,
and the king of glory shall come in.
Who is this king of glory?
The God of armies, he is the king of glory.

O God, I will lift my soul to you.
I have trusted you, God, do not let me be shamed,
do not leave my enemies to triumph over me.
No one who waits and hopes for you will be shamed,
but those who lose faith without reason will be ashamed.
God, make me know your ways, teach me your paths.
Make my steps tread on truth because you are the God of
my salvation,
I have waited for you all day long.
O God, remember your sweet mercy and your goodness
since long ago.
Forget the sins of my youth and all my offences, but
remember me according to your goodness,
because you are generous, O God.
God is good and straight,
and so he will teach sinners the way.
He will guide the poor in judgement
and teach the poor his own way.
All his paths are goodness and truth
to those who keep the conditions of his agreement and his
sayings.
O God, forgive me my wickedness because of your name,
because I am very wicked.
Who fears God? He will instruct him in the way of his
choice.
His soul will rest in a good place
and his descendants will inherit the land.
The secret thoughts of God are for those that fear him:
he will tell them the conditions of his agreement.

My eyes look for God continually
because he will untangle my feet from the net.
Turn your face to me and favour me
because I am alone and poor.
The distress of my heart is very great,
bring me out from my distress.
See my suffering and my labour
and forgive me all my sins.
See my enemies, they are many
and they have hated me with violence.
Keep my soul and save me, do not let me be shamed,
I have taken refuge in you.
Honesty and uprightness will preserve me
because I have waited for you.
O God, set Israel free from his distress.

Judge me, God,
I have been honest in my life;
my confidence is in God and I shall not falter.
Test me, God, and try me,
examine my bowels and my heart.
Your goodness was in my eyes
and I have lived by your truthfulness.
I have not sat among men that loved vanity
and I will not go with liars.
I will wash my hands in innocence and come to your altar,
   O God,
and make my voice be heard in thanksgiving
and declare aloud all your wonderful actions.
O God, I have loved your house and the place where your
   glory is.
Do not count my soul among sinners or my life among
   bloody and violent men,
who have cunning in their hands and a bribe in their right
   hand.
I will be honest in my life:
save me and be good to me.
My feet stand on level ground;
I shall bless God in the assemblies.

God is my light and my salvation; who shall I fear?

God is the strong castle of my life; who will make me afraid?

The wicked and my enemies came against me, they were ready to devour my flesh,

but they stumbled and fell down.

If an army encamped comes out against me my heart will not be afraid,

if war comes against me, this is my confidence.

I have asked one thing from God and that is my desire:

that I should live in the house of God all my days,

and see and enjoy God and look for him in his temple.

On the day of evil he will take me into his house,

he will hide me in his tent,

he will lift me up onto a high rock.

And at that time my head shall be lifted up above my enemies around me,

and I will sacrifice in his tent with the sound of trumpets;

I will sing and make music to God.

God, hear my voice when I cry out,

favour me and answer me.

My heart spoke to you, look for my face;

O God, I will look for your face.

Do not hide your face,

do not be angry or turn away your servant.

You have been my help, do not leave me alone,

do not desert me, O God of my salvation.

Even if my father and my mother desert me, God will take me in.

God, teach me your way, and lead me on an easy path,
because my enemies are watching for me.
Do not leave me to the bad will of my enemies,
their declarations are false and their breath is violence.
But I believe
and I shall see the goodness of God in the land of the living.
O wait for God, be strong, have a strong heart;
and wait for God.

O God, I shall cry out to you;
my rock, do not be silent,
because if you are quiet I shall be like those who fall down
  into the pit.
Listen to the voice of my prayers when I cry out to you,
when I raise up my hands towards your holy roof.
Do not take me away with the wicked and with those that
  do injustices,
who talk peace to their neighbours and have evil in their
  hearts.
Pay those men according to their actions and their evil
  practices;
pay them according to the work of their hands,
pay them as they have deserved.
They will not consider the acts of God or the work of the
  hands of God;
he shall tumble them down, he shall not build them up.
I bless God, because he heard the voice of my prayers.
God is my strength and my shield:
the confidence of my heart was in him and I was helped,
I triumphed in my heart, and I shall thank him with singing.
God is our strength,
he is the strong fortress that saves his anointed one.
Save your people, bless your inheritance,
feed them and carry them for ever.

Praise God, sons of gods;
give glory and strength to God.
Give God the name of his glory,
bow down to God in the majesty of his holiness.
The voice of God over the water:
the glory of God has made thunder,
God over the masses of the water.
The voice of God is strength, his voice is majesty.
The voice of God is the breaking down of a forest of cedars:
God breaks down the cedars of Lebanon.
He has made the mountains skip like calves,
Lebanon and Sirion like young wild oxen.
The voice of God strikes out fire;
the voice of God will put the desert in the pains of
    childbirth,
God will make the desert of Kadesh agonize.
The voice of God will put the cattle in birth pains
and strip the forest bare.
And everything says Glory in his temple.
God has put his seat on the flood of water,
he is king on his throne for ever.
God shall give strength to his people,
God shall bless his people with peace.

I will praise you, God, because you have lifted me up,
and you have not made my enemies be glad against me.
God, my God, I have cried out to you and you healed me.
O God, you have brought up my soul out of hell,
and made me live and not go down into the pit.
Sing with music to God, you saints,
and remember his holiness with thanksgiving.
His anger is a moment, but his grace is life;
in the evening we shall weep, but in the morning we shall
    shout for joy.
I said in my happiness, I shall never fall down.
God, in your grace you made me stand on strength like a
    mountain,
you hid your face and I was troubled.
O God, I will cry out to you, I will pray to God.
What profit is there in my blood, if I fall into the ditch?
Will dust thank you? Will it say you were faithful?
Hear me, God, and favour me; O God, help me.
You have turned my lamentations into dancing,
you have taken off my sackcloth and dressed me in gladness,
so that my spirit may sing to you and not be silent.
God, my God, I will thank you for ever.

O God, you are my refuge, let me never be ashamed:
save me in your justice.
Listen to me and save me quickly,
be the crag of my strength and my fortress to save me.
You are my rock and my fortress,
you shall guide me and lead me because of your name.
You will bring me out of the net they have hidden to
  entangle me,
because you are my refuge.
I shall give my spirit into your hands,
you saved me, O God, truthful God.
I have hated empty idolatry and I have hoped in God.
I will be glad and rejoice because of your mercy;
you have seen my affliction and penetrated the sufferings of
  my soul.
You did not hand me over to my enemies,
but you set my feet to walk in a broad and open place.
Be good to me, God, because I am very much troubled;
my eyes and my soul and my body are eaten up with
  misery.
Grief has eaten up my life, groans have eaten away years.
My strength has run out because of my wickedness, and my
  bones are eaten away.
My name has become a curse-word to my enemies, and to
  my neighbours most of all;
those who know me are afraid when they hear my name.
I have been forgotten like a dead man who is not considered,
like a pot that was broken;
I have heard the whispering of a crowd, there was terror
  round me;

they made plans against me, they conspired to take my soul.
O God, I hoped in you, I said, You are my God.
At all times I am in your hands,
save me from my enemies and my persecutors.
Make your face a bright light to your servant,
save me by your mercy.
O God, do not let me be ashamed, because I have cried out
to you.
The wicked shall be shamed, they shall be silent in hell.
The tongue of deceit that speaks arrogance and pride and
contempt against the just man shall be struck dumb.
How very great your merciful goodness is,
which you have hidden for those who fear you,
which you exercise for those who run to you from the sons
of Adam.
You shall hide them from the snares of men in the hiding
place of your presence,
you shall hide them in your house from angry tongues.
I bless God because he has been wonderfully good to me in
a besieged city.
I said in my great fear, I have been taken away from the
sight of your eyes;
surely you heard the voice of my prayers when I cried out
to you.
Love God, all you who are his saints;
God saves the faithful, he pays the proud man with an
abundant payment.
Be strong, have courage in your heart, everyone who hopes
in God.

Happy is the man whose wickedness is forgiven,
whose sins are covered up.
Happy is that man:
God will find no evil in him, there is no falsity in his soul.
When I was silent, my bones withered away with groaning
    all day long.
Your hand was heavy on me day and night,
my moisture dried up like a drought in the hot season.
I will show you my sin, I have not covered my wickedness.
I said, I will confess my sins to God,
and so you forgave the wickedness of my sin.
Therefore everyone who is holy shall pray to you in his
    time,
and in the great flood the water shall not reach him.
You are my hiding-place, you will protect me from trouble,
and there shall be shouts of freedom all around me.
I will instruct you and teach you the way you are to go.
I will advise you and watch you.
Do not be like the horse or the mule that understand
    nothing,
and their mouth must be held with a bit and bridle or they
    run loose.
The wicked man has many sorrows,
the man who hopes in God is surrounded with mercy and
    goodness.
Rejoice in God and be very glad, you just;
shout with joy, all who are upright in their hearts.

Rejoice in God, you just,
because his praise is becoming to honest men.
Give thanks to God with music on the harp,
sing to him with music on the double-stringed harp.
Sing him a new song,
play well and very loudly.
Because the words of God are honest and his work is
   faithful:
he loves justice and judgement,
the earth is full of the merciful goodness of God.
The word of God built heaven,
the breath of his mouth made the army of heaven.
He gathers the water of the sea into a heap,
and he puts away deep water in a store-house.
The whole earth shall be afraid because of God,
all the people in the world shall be afraid because of him.
Because he spoke, and it was;
he commanded, and it stood.
God has made the thoughts of the nations nonsense;
he has frustrated the ideas of peoples.
The thoughts of God shall stand for ever,
the thoughts of his heart in every generation.
Happy is the nation whose God is God,
and the people he chooses to be his possession.
God looked out of heaven and he saw all the sons of Adam,
he looked from the place where he is at everyone who lived
   on the earth.
God makes their hearts, he understands all their actions.
A king is not protected by the size of an army,
nor will a very strong man be saved by great strength.

Horses are deceiving, they do not save,
the greatness of the power of horses will not save.
But look: the eyes of God are on those that fear him,
on those that trust his goodness;
to save their souls from death,
and to make them live in a time of famine.
Our souls have waited for God,
he is our help and our shield.
We shall be glad in our hearts because of him,
because our confidence has been in his name and in his
    holiness.
O God, your mercy is over us,
because we trusted you.

I shall bless God in every season,
and his praises will be always in my mouth.
My soul will glory in God, let the poor hear and be glad.
Praise God with me, we shall glorify his name together.
I looked for God and he answered me,
and rescued me out of all my fears.
They looked to him and they became shining like a light;
their faces will not be ashamed.
A poor man cried out and God heard him
and rescued him out of all his miseries.
The angel of God has made his camp around those that fear
    God,
and he saves them.
Taste and see that God is good.
Happy is the man who takes refuge in him.
Fear God, you holy ones;
those that fear him shall not want.
The whelps of lions shall hunger and go wanting,
but those who look for God shall not want for any good
    thing.
Come, my sons, listen to me,
and I will teach you the fear of God.
Who desires life and loves to see good days?
Keep your tongue from evil, keep your lips from deceit.
Avoid evil and do good, search for peace and run after it.
The eyes of God are on the just, he hears them calling;
God has set his face against those that do evil,
to wipe away their memory from the earth.
They cried out and God heard them,
and rescued them out of all their miseries.

God is close to the broken-hearted,
he saves the crushed in spirit.
The just man has many sufferings,
and God will rescue him out of all of them.
God keeps all his bones and none of them is broken.
The evil of the wicked man shall be his death,
and those that have hated the just man shall be found guilty.
God sets free the souls of his servants,
and no one of those who run to him shall be found guilty.

O God, accuse my accusers,
and fight against those who fight against me.
Take arms and a shield
and rise up and help me.
Take a spear,
shut the road against those who run after me.
Say to my soul, I am your salvation.
Those who hunted my soul shall be confused and ashamed,
those who devised harm against me shall be turned back and
    abashed.
They shall be like chaff on the wind
and the angel of God shall winnow them,
their road shall be dark and slippery
and the angel of God shall run after them;
because they made a pit and hid their net against me with-
    out reason,
they dug against my life without reason.
Destruction shall come to them suddenly,
they shall be caught in the net that they hid,
they shall fall and be destroyed.
My soul will rejoice in God and be glad because he has
    saved me.
My bones will say, O God, who is like you?
To save the poor man from one that is stronger,
to save the poor and wretched man from one that strips him
    bare.
Violent witnesses appeared against me
to demand things of which I knew nothing,
to pay evil for good, to take away my life.
But when they were sick I wore sackcloth,
I afflicted my soul with fasting and prayed in my heart.

As if it had been my friend and my brother;
and I bowed my head and was sad as if it had been my
mother.
When I stumbled they were glad and met together,
bad men met together against me and I did not know.
They tore me apart, they were not silent.
They broke me with their teeth like a cake,
with profanity and mocking.
O God, how long will you watch this?
Rescue my soul from griefs, and my life from young lions.
I will thank you in a great assembly.
I will praise you in a strong nation.
Do not let my enemies boast against me untruly,
or those that hate me for no reason wink about me.
They will not speak peace,
they invent speeches of deceit against quiet people.
They opened their mouths against me:
they said, Well, well, we can see.
O God, you have seen this; do not be silent, O God.
Rouse up and awake: God, come to judgement, God, hear
my case.
Do not let them boast over me, saying in their hearts,
Here is the desire of our souls.
Do not let them say, We have devoured him.
Those that were glad of my harm shall be ashamed and
confused.
Those that boasted against me shall be dressed in shame and
disgrace.
But those that were delighted because of my justice shall be
glad and shout for joy.
They shall cry out continually, God is great,
and he is pleased with the gladness of his servant.
And my tongue shall meditate your justice and your praises
all the day long.

Sin speaks to the wicked man in his heart,
the fear of God is not in his sight,
he has flattered himself in his own eyes
that his wickedness will not be found out, it is not abomin-
   able.
But the language in his mouth is wickedness and deceit,
he has given up understanding and doing good.
He will dream up wickedness in his bed,
he will set himself on a wrong way,
he will not refuse evil.
O God, your goodness is in heaven,
your faithfulness is as wide as the sky.
Your justice is like the mountains of God
and your judgements are a very deep place.
O God, you save men and beasts.
O God, how precious your mercy is,
and the sons of Adam shall run in under the shadow of your
   wings.
They shall be satisfied with the riches of your house,
you shall make them drink from the streams of your
   pleasures.
Because the springs of life are with you,
and in your light we shall see light.
Make your mercy and goodness continual to those that
   know you,
and your justice to the upright in heart.
Do not let men that walk proudly come near me,
or men with wicked hands come after me.
Those that commit wickedness have fallen,
they have been thrown down and they cannot rise.

Do not disturb yourself about the wicked,
do not be jealous of those that do injustices.
They will wither quickly like grass,
and wither away like the green of young grass.
Trust God and do good,
live on the earth and be faithful.
Be delighted with God,
he will give you what you ask for in your heart.
Throw your path on God, and trust him,
and he will do it.
He will lift up your justice like the light and your rights like
    the midday.
Be quiet, wait for God, be patient;
do not disturb yourself about a prosperous man
or a man who plans to do wrong and succeeds.
Be quiet and not angry, leave rage alone,
do not disturb yourself simply to do wrong.
The wicked will be taken away,
and those who wait for God will inherit the earth.
A little longer and the wicked man will be gone,
you will think of the place where he was and not find it.
And the poor will inherit the earth
and they shall enjoy a great peace.
The wicked man plots against the just man,
he snaps at him with his teeth.
God will laugh at him,
because he has seen that his day will come.
The wicked have taken swords and bent bows to strike
    down the poor and wretched
and to murder those that proceed honestly.

Their swords will stick in their own hearts
and their bows will be broken.
The little power of the honest man is better than the abun-
    dance of the wicked
because the weapons of the wicked will be broken
and God keeps the just.
God knows honest men and their life,
and their inheritance is lasting.
They will not be shamed in an evil season,
in times of famine they will have enough.
The wicked will perish,
the enemies of God will waste like the greenness of pastures,
they shall waste away like smoke.
The wicked man borrows and does not repay,
but the just man is generous and gives.
Those that he blesses shall inherit the earth,
and those he curses shall be destroyed.
God guides a man's steps and delights in his path.
Although he stumbles he will not fall down
because God takes him by the hand.
I was young and have grown old,
and I have not seen a just man deserted and his children
    begging their bread.
He is generous and lends all the day long,
and his children are his blessing.
Leave evil and do good, and live for ever.
Because God loves justice and he will not desert his holy
    ones:
he keeps them for ever,
but the children of the wicked perish.
Just men shall inherit the earth
and live on it for ever.

Their mouths will meditate wisdom
and their tongues will speak justice.
The laws of their God will be in their heart
and they shall never stumble on their paths.
The wicked man watches the upright,
he looks for a way to murder him,
but God will not leave him in his hands
and will not condemn him when he is judged.
Wait for God, keep to his way,
and he will raise you up to inherit the earth:
you shall see this in the destruction of the wicked.
I have seen a wicked man without mercy,
spreading himself like a branching tree which is well rooted;
but he went, now he is not there,
I looked for him and he could not be found.
See the honest and the upright man:
the man of peace has his posterity.
And the sinners are all destroyed together,
the wicked are taken away before the end.
God saves the just:
he is their refuge in the time of trouble.
God helps them and rescues them;
he will rescue them from the wicked and will save them,
because he was their refuge.

38

O God, do not rebuke me angrily
or punish me very angrily.
Your arrows have sunk into me, your hand has come down
    on me,
there is no soundness in my body, because of your indig-
    nation,
there is no health in my bones, because I have sinned.
My wickedness is over my head,
it is a heavy load, I cannot carry it.
My bruises stink and fester because of my foolishness.
I have bent down, I have bowed down deeply,
I have walked in great sadness all day long.
My loins are burning, there is no soundness in my body.
I am humbled and very much broken,
I have groaned because my heart roared.
O God, my desire is in your sight
and my groaning was not hidden from you.
My heart is panting,
and my powers have left me,
and the light of my eyes has gone out.
My loving friends and my companions keep from me
    because I was struck down,
and my kin keep far off.
The enemies of my soul have made traps,
those who desire evil to me have spoken of death,
they ruminate deceits all day.
I shall be deaf and not hear,
I shall be dumb and shall not open my mouth.
I was like a man who hears nothing,
and there are no reproaches on his lips.

Because I have trusted you, God,
you will answer, my lord and my God.
I said that they should not triumph over me
or boast because my feet stumble.
But I am near to falling down, I am continually in pain.
I will confess the injustice I have done,
I will trouble myself over my sins.
My enemies have become strong in their lives,
and those that hate me unjustly have become very many.
Those that pay back evil for good are against me
because I follow good.
O God my God, do not leave me alone,
do not be distant from me.
Come quickly to help me, my lord and my salvation.

39

I said, I will keep from sinning in my words,
I will put a bridle on my mouth in the presence of an unjust
    man.
I was dumb and silent, I kept peace without comfort,
I was stirred up to pain and grief.
My heart was hot in me, fire burned in my thoughts,
and I have spoken.
God makes me know my death, and the number of my days;
I will study my fragility.
My days are inches, my time is a nothing in your eyes.
Surely every man living is vanity.
Surely a man walks like a ghost,
and his disturbance is vanity.
He gathers wealth and does not know who shall have it.
God, what have I waited for? My hope is with you.
Save me from all my sins,
do not leave me to be laughed at by fools.
I am dumb, I will not open my mouth,
because you have done it.
Take the striking of your hand away from me,
I am dying of the unfriendliness of your hand.
When you have punished man with rebukes against his
    wickedness,
you have torn away his beauty like a moth:
every man is mere vanity.
Hear my prayers, O God, listen to my cries.
Do not be silent at my tears,
because I am a guest with you,
I am a traveller like all my fathers.
Turn your eyes away from me,
so that I am comforted before I depart and die.

40

I waited, I waited for God,
and he turned to me and heard my voice.
He brought me up out of a pit of groaning, out of mud and
dirt.
He put my feet on a crag and made me walk steadily.
He put a new song into my mouth, the praises of our God;
and many shall see and be afraid and trust God.
O, the blessings of the man whose confidence is in God,
who has not depended on the proud nor on deceivers.
O God my God, very many times you have been wonderful
in your working and in your devices over us,
there is no one to compare to you,
although I shall tell and declare them,
they are more than I can say.
You were not placated by sacrifices and offerings,
only your ears were open,
you did not demand burnt offerings nor offerings for sin.
I said, I have come.
This is written about me in the book:
I have been delighted to do your pleasure, O my God,
and your law is written in my body.
I have declared justice in the great assembly, I will not be
silent,
O God you know this.
I have not hidden your justice in my heart.
I have declared that you are faithful and save.
I have not hidden your goodness or your truthfulness from
the great assembly.
O God, you will not keep your merciful kindnesses from
me,

your mercy and your truthfulness will be my continual
   protection.
Because I am surrounded by evils, I can no longer number
   them,
my injustices have overtaken me, I cannot see beyond them.
They are more numerous than the hairs on my head,
and my heart has failed me.
O God be pleased to save me, God be quick to help me.
Those that seek out my soul to destroy it shall be ashamed
   and confused;
those that take pleasure in my harm shall be thrown back
   and shamed.
Those that say to me, Aha! Aha! shall be ruined because of
   their shame.
But those that look for God shall be glad and joyful over
   you.
Those that love your salvation will say continually, Praise
   God.
And I am poor and destitute, God will think of me.
You are my helper and my rescuer,
O God do not be long.

41

Happy is the man who considers the poor:
God will save him on the bad day.
May God help him and make him live and be happy on
    earth,
and not leave him to the will of his enemies.
God will lift him up from the bed of his weakness,
and he will take away his infirmity when he is sick.
I said, God be good to me, heal my soul
because I have sinned against you.
My enemies speak wickedly to me.
When will he die and his name be wiped out?
The man that comes to see me talks without meaning,
his heart gathers wickedness,
he goes out and he talks.
Those that hate me whisper against me all together,
they make plots against me:
There is a curse on him,
when he lies down he will never rise again.
And my friend whom I trusted, who had eaten my bread,
has put out his foot to kick me.
God, be good to me, raise me up, and I shall pay them.
Now I know that you delight in me,
because my enemies will not boast over me.
I was honest and you held me up
and made me stand in your presence for ever.
Bless God, who is the God of Israel,
from for ever until for ever.
Amen and amen.

God, as the deer pant for the rivers so my soul pants after
  you.

My soul has thirsted for God, for a living God.

When shall I come and appear before God?

My tears were my bread day and night,

when they said to me all day, Where is your God?

I will remember this, I will pour out my soul to myself:

I shall go in the crowd,

I shall walk with them to the house of God,

with shouting and thanksgiving in the loud noise of the
  festival.

My soul, why are you cast down, why do you disturb
  yourself?

Trust God, because I will still thank him, his face saves.

O my God, because my soul is cast down in me,

therefore I will remember you in the country of Jordan,

and in Hermon, and at mount Mizar.

Deep calls to deep at the voice of your waterfalls,

your waves and your floods have travelled over me,

In the day God commands his goodness,

and in the night his song is with me,

to pray to the God of my life.

I will say to God my rock, Why have you forgotten me?

Why do I go sadly and my enemies persecute me?

My bones are broken to bits and my enemies have insulted
  me,

saying all day long, Where is your God?

My soul, why are you cast down, why are you disturbed?

Trust God, because I will still thank him,

his face saves, he is my God.

43

Judge me, God, and argue my case with a people that is not
     holy.
Save me from a deceitful and a wicked man.
Because you are the God of my endurance;
why have you left me alone?
Why do I go sadly and my enemies persecute me?
Send out your light and your truth,
which will guide me and bring me to your holy hill
and into the place where you are.
And I will go to the altar of God,
to the God of my gladness and my joy,
and give thanks to God, who is my God, with the music of
     a harp.
My soul, why are you cast down and troubled?
Trust God, because I will still thank him,
his face saves, he is my God.

O God, we have listened and heard,
and our fathers have told us what you did in their day, in
    the past time.
You dispossessed nations with your hand, and planted our
    fathers,
you destroyed peoples, and spread out our fathers.
Because it was not their swords that took the land,
it was not their arm that saved them,
but your arm and your right hand and the light of your
    face,
because you favoured them.
It is you, God, you are my king,
commander of the miracles of Jacob.
Through you we shall throw down our enemies,
and in your name we shall trample on those that are against
    us.
Because I shall not trust my bow, and my sword will not
    save me,
but you have rescued us from our enemies
and shamed those that hate us.
Because of God we have boasted all day long,
we shall thank him for ever.
You have left us alone and made us ashamed,
because you will not go into battle with our armies.
You turn us back from our enemies,
and those that hate us have taken the spoils of war.
You have left us like sheep to be eaten up,
we were strong among the nations but you have scattered
    us.
You will sell away your people without a price,

there is no profit or payment.
You have made us the bad joke of our neighbours,
to be mocked and despised by everyone around us.
You have made us a proverb among foreign nations,
and the peoples shake their heads at us.
All day long I see my dishonour,
my face is ashamed and shame has covered me,
because of the mocking and the blasphemous voice,
because of my enemy and because of his revenge.
All this has come to us, and we have not forgotten you:
we have not gone back on your agreement.
Our hearts have not turned back,
nor have our steps gone aside from your way,
because you crushed us among jackals
and covered us with the shadows of death.
If we forgot the name of God, if we held out our hands to
    any foreign god,
will God not discover it?
Because he knows what is hidden in the heart.
And because of you we have been massacred all day long,
we have been counted like sheep to be slaughtered.
O God, awake, why are you sleeping?
Wake, do not leave us for ever.
Why do you hide your face?
Will you forget our persecutions and afflictions?
Because our souls have been bowed down into the dust,
and our bodies have stuck to the earth, face downwards.
Rise up and help us, take us back because of your mercy.

My heart has been stirred up with a good thought:
I utter my songs to the king.
My tongue is like the pen of a writer writing quickly.
You are better in beauty than the children of men,
and grace is poured out on your lips,
and therefore God has blessed you for ever.
Strong one, tie your sword on your thigh,
and your greatness and your gloriousness.
Ride out, achieve and be glorious about truth and poverty
    and justice,
and your right hand will tell you terrible things.
Your arrows have been sharpened
and the peoples fall down under you
and the hearts of the king's enemies faint.
O God, your throne is for ever and ever,
and the sceptre of your kingdom is the sceptre of justice.
You have loved justice and hated wickedness,
and God who is your God has anointed you with the oil of
    gladness above your companions.
There is myrrh and aloes and cassia on your clothing,
and you hear the music of harps in palaces of ivory.
The daughter of kings is among your women,
the queen stands at your right hand wearing fine gold from
    Ophir.
My daughter listen and see this: attend to me:
forget your nation and your father's house,
and the king will greatly desire your beauty;
    he is your lord, bow down to him.
The daughter of Tyre will bring her gift,
and the richest of the people will ask for your favour.

The daughter of the king is all glorious,
her dress is embroidered with gold.
She shall be brought in to the king dressed in colours,
her virgin companions shall follow her.
They shall be brought with gladness and joy,
and they shall go into the king's house.
Instead of your fathers you shall have sons,
you shall make them princes over the whole earth.
I will tell your name to every generation,
and nations will thank you for ever and ever.

God is our refuge and our strength,
and a help in trouble ready to be found.
We shall not be afraid if the earth moves
and the mountains fall down into the deepest part of the
    sea,
even though the sea should swell and be boisterous,
and the mountains shivered.
But the running of the river will gladden the city of God,
and the holy place which is the house of the most high.
God is in the middle of the city and it shall not be troubled,
God will come to help them with the break of day.
Nations are troubled and kingdoms shaken,
he utters his voice and the earth dissolves.
The God of armies is with us,
the God of Jacob is our mountain castle.
Come and see the works of God, he has made ruins on the
    earth.
He stops wars as far as the ends of the earth,
he will break the bow and snap the spear,
he will burn chariots with a fire.
Be quiet, and know that I am God.
I will triumph among nations, I will triumph on the earth.
The God of armies is with us,
the God of Jacob is our mountain castle.

47

Clap your hands, all you peoples,
shout joyfully to God with a loud noise,
because God is most high and terrible,
and a king who is strong over the whole earth.
He will put peoples under us and nations under our feet.
He has chosen an inheritance for us:
the glory of Jacob whom he loved.
God has gone up with a joyful noise
and with the sound of trumpets.
Sing to God with the harp, sing to him with the harp,
sing to our king with the harp, sing to him with the harp.
God is the king of the whole earth, sing to him with the
    harp played skilfully.
God is the king of nations,
he has sat down in his throne, which is holy.
The princes of peoples have gathered,
the people of the God of Abraham,
the shields of the world belong to him,
and he is very high.

God is great, praise him,
praise him in the city of our God and on his holy hill.
Mount Zion is a fine hill, the joy of the whole world:
the north mountain, the city of the great king.
God is a mountain refuge,
he is known in the houses of Zion.
See, the kings came together and passed by;
they stared and were amazed,
they were troubled and they hurried away.
They began to tremble, they agonized like a woman in
    childbirth;
you have broken up the ships of Tarshish with an east wind.
We saw it happen as we heard it said,
in the city of the God of armies,
in the city of our God.
God will make the city steady for ever.
O God, we have remembered your mercy in your temple.
O God, your praise is like your name,
it reaches to the ends of the earth,
and your right hand is full of justice.
Mount Zion shall be glad
and the daughters of Judah shall be very glad because of
    your judgements.
Go around Zion, pass round her in a circle,
count her towers, consider the walls in your heart,
move among the houses and tell it to a later generation.
This is the God who is our God, for ever and ever.
And he will guide us for ever.

Hear this, all people, listen, every man alive in this time,
sons of Adam, sons of men, rich and poor:
my mouth will speak wisdom and my heart meditate
  understanding.
I will hear a parable,
I will speak a dark language with the music of a harp.
Why should I be afraid in evil times?
Shall I be surrounded by the injustices of my enemies,
by those who trust their wealth
and are proud of the quantity of their possessions?
A brother cannot ransom his brother, he cannot pay God
  for him.
The ransom for his soul will be a high price,
it will never be enough to let him live forever
and never see the grave.
But he will see it. Wise men will die,
and the brute and the fool will also perish
and leave their wealth to others.
In their imagination their houses stand for ever,
they are lived in from generation to generation.
They have named their land after their own names.
But man will not continue in honour,
he is like the cattle, they die.
The way of these men is foolishness,
those who come after them will eat and be happy.
They go down like sheep to hell and death is their shepherd,
when morning comes honest men are their masters.
Their shape is for consuming, they go to hell from their
  houses.

But God will ransom my soul from hell, because he will
  take me.
Do not be afraid when a man becomes rich
and the gloriousness of his house increases.
When he dies he shall not take away anything,
and his greatness will not descend with him.
Even though he thought himself happy in his life,
and if you do good to yourself they praise you,
he will go back to the generations of his fathers
and never see the light.
Man will not continue in honour,
he is like the cattle, and they die.

God, God is God:
God spoke and summoned the world,
from the sun's rising place to its setting place.
God shone from Zion in perfect beauty.
Our God is coming and he will not be silent.
Burning fire will be in front of him
and a great tempest all around him.
He will summon heaven and earth to judge his people.
Gather up my holy ones
who have sworn to my agreement with a sacrifice.
Heaven declares his justice, because God himself is judge.
Listen, my people, and I will speak;
Israel, I will protest against you;
I am God, I am your God.
I will not rebuke you for your sacrifices and your burnt
    offerings
which I see continually.
I shall not receive a bull from your shed
or a billy-goat from your flock,
because every beast in the forest
and the wild birds on a thousand mountains are mine.
I know every bird that flies in the mountains,
and every country animal is in my sight.
If I am hungry I will not tell you,
because the world and its fullness are mine.
Shall I eat the meat of bulls
and drink the blood of billy-goats?
Give God the sacrifice of thanksgiving:
pay the most high God your promises,
and cry out to me on the day of disaster,

and I shall save you and you will honour me.
God said to the unjust man,
Why should you declare my laws,
and take my agreements into your mouth?
You have hated discipline,
and thrown down my words behind you.
When you saw a thief you were pleased with him,
and you stand among adulterers.
You opened your mouth in wickedness
and your tongue was the instrument of deceit.
You sit to speak against your brother,
you slander your own mother's son.
You have done this and I was silent
and you thought that I was like you.
I will rebuke you, I will make you see the truth.
Consider this, you who forget God,
for fear I should break you to pieces,
and there is no one to save you.
I am honoured in the sacrifice of thanksgiving.
I will bring the man who has chosen his way
to see the salvation of God.

God have mercy on me because of your goodness,
and because of the great number of your mercies take away
    my offences.
Wash me thoroughly from my wickedness, clean my sin.
I know my offences well, and I see my sin continually.
I have sinned against you, I have sinned only against you,
I have done evil in your sight,
to prove that your words will be just
and your judgement will be truthful.
And I was born in wickedness,
and my mother conceived me in sin.
But you have loved the truth in dark places,
you will show me wisdom in a mystery;
sprinkle me with a brush of herbs and I shall be clean,
wash me and I shall be whiter than snow.
You will make my ears hear noises of joy and gladness,
and the bones you have crushed will rejoice.
Turn away your face from my sins and take away my
    offence.
O God, make me a clean heart, and renew a strong spirit in
    me.
Do not chase me away from your presence,
do not take your holy spirit from me.
Give me back the gladness of your salvation
and steady me with a willing spirit.
I will teach your ways to those that have offended,
and sinners will turn back to you.
Save me from blood, O God, God of my salvation;
my tongue will shout and sing your justice.
O God, you will open my lips,

and my mouth will announce your praises.
Because you will not be pleased with sacrifice,
or I should give it,
you will not want a burnt offering.
The sacrifice of God is a broken spirit;
O God, you will not despise a broken and crushed heart.
Be good to Zion in your kindness,
you will build up the walls of Jerusalem.
Then you will be pleased with the sacrifices of justice,
the grilled and the burnt offerings,
then they will offer young bulls on your altar.

52

Great man, why do you boast about your wickedness?
God is merciful all day long.
Your tongue is a deadly instrument,
sharp as a razor and deceitful.
You have loved evil more than good
and lying more than speaking the truth.
Deceitful tongue, you have loved every deadly word.
And God will ruin you for ever,
he will take you and pull you out of your tent,
and tear up your roots from the land of the living.
The just shall see this and be afraid,
and they shall laugh at you.
Look at the man who will not take God for his fortress,
he trusted the quantity of his possessions,
his strength was in his wickedness.
But I am like an olive tree that grows branches in the house
    of God.
I have trusted the mercy of God for ever and ever.
I will thank you for ever, because you have done this,
and I will hope because of your name, because it is very
    good, with all your holy ones.

The fool has said in his heart, There is no God.
They are corrupt, they have done abominable things,
no one does good.
God looked down from heaven at the sons of Adam
to see if there was anyone who understood and who looked
  for God.
They have all turned aside and every one of them has be-
  come filthy;
and no one does good, not one of them.
Those criminals have eaten my people like they eat bread,
and did they not know?
They have not cried out to God.
They were very much afraid, where there was nothing to
  fear,
because God has scattered the bones of the enemy that made
  his camp against you;
you have made them ashamed because God rejected them.
Who will come from Zion to save Israel?
When God has reversed the captivity of his people
then Jacob shall be full of gladness and Israel full of pleasure.

54

O God, save me by your name, and justify me by your
 power.
O God, hear my prayer, listen to the words of my mouth.
Strangers have stood up against me,
and violent men have hunted for my life,
they have not considered God.
Look, God is helping me, my God is protecting my life;
may evil turn on those who watch out against me;
be true and destroy them.
I will sacrifice in freedom,
I will thank the name of God because it is good:
because he has rescued me from all trouble
and I have looked scornfully at my enemies.

God, hear my prayer, do not hide from my prayer;
listen and answer me.
I am disturbed, I lament and cry out,
because of the voice of my enemy,
because of the persecution of injustice,
because they will deal with me wickedly,
and with anger and with hatred.
My heart is painful in my body
and the terrors of death have descended on me.
I am afraid and shivering, I am full of horror.
And I said, Who will give me wings like a dove?
I will fly away and find a place.
I will fly far away,
I will find a place in the wild country.
I will escape quickly from the storm-wind and the tempest.
O God, scatter and divide their voices.
In this city I have seen violence and division:
they are round it day and night, sitting on its walls,
and wickedness and injustice are in the middle of it.
Destruction is in the middle of it,
oppression and deceit live in its market-place.
It was not an enemy that spoke against me,
or I would bear it;
it was not one who hated me that was strong against me,
or I would hide from him;
but it was you my equal and my companion and my friend,
with whom I had pleasant conversation,
and walked among many people in the house of God.
Let death overtake them,
let them drop living into hell,

because where they live evil is in the middle of them.
I shall cry to God and he will save me.
At sunset and at dawn and at midday I shall lament and cry
   out,
and he has heard my voice.
He has set free my spirit in peace from the war that was
   fought against me;
they were many against me.
God heard and he answered them,
sitting in his ancient place.
They suffer no changes, they have no fear of God.
A man puts out his hand against a friend,
he breaks his agreements,
the words in his mouth are as smooth as butter
and war is in his heart:
his words are softer than oil
and like drawn swords.
Put your trust in God and he will care for you,
he will not let the just man stumble for ever.
God, bring them down into the pit of death;
men of bloody violence and deceit shall not see half their
   days.
I trust you, God.

God be merciful to me, because man is breathless against
    me,
he fights all the day long, he persecutes me.
All the day long my enemies are breathless against me,
many proud fighters.
On the day of my great fear I shall be confident in you:
in God whose words I praise.
I have trusted in God and I shall not be afraid:
what can flesh and bone do to me?
They will twist my words all day long,
all their thoughts are for evil against me.
They gather together, they hide themselves,
they track my footprints,
they hunt for my life.
Reward them for that evil;
be angry, God, and bring down the peoples.
You have measured my wanderings;
then put my tears into your tear-bottle.
Are they not written in your book?
On the day when I cry out my enemies shall turn away;
I know this: God is on my side.
In God, whose words I praise;
in the God whose words I praise.
I have trusted in God, I shall not be afraid:
what can man do to me?
My vows are on my head, O God,
I will pay you offerings of thanks.
You have saved my spirit from death,
and surely saved my feet from stumbling;
to walk in God's presence in the light of the living.

Be merciful to me, O God, be merciful to me,
because you are the refuge of my spirit,
and I will shelter under the shadows of your wings
until destruction passes.
I will call out to the most high God,
to God who works strongly over me.
He will send out of heaven and save me,
he has rebuked those that hunted me and panted.
God will send out his love and his truth.
My soul is among lions;
I must lie down among the sons of man, they are on fire,
their teeth are a spear and arrows,
their tongue is a sharp sword.
O God, be high above the heavens,
and your glory over the whole earth.
They put a net to trip my feet, and my spirit is bowed down.
They dug a pit in my path, and fell down into it.
My heart is steady, O God, my heart is steady;
I will sing and give praise.
Wake my glory, wake the lyre and the harp,
I will wake the dawn and give thanks to you, O God,
    among the peoples.
I will sing with the harp among the nations.
Because your love is like the heavens
and your truth is like the sky.
O God, be high above the heavens,
and your glory over the whole earth.

O you mighty, do you speak the truth?
You sons of man, do you judge honestly?
You do wrong in your hearts,
and your hands measure out injustices on the earth.
The bad were born crooked,
the liars turned wrong in the womb.
They are poisonous like snakes,
and deaf like an adder that stops up its ears:
it will not hear the whisper of wise magic.
God, break their teeth in their mouths.
God, tear out the great teeth of the young lions.
They will disappear like water,
they will vanish while he aims his arrows.
Like a snail that melts as it moves,
like a woman's abortion that never saw sunlight.
Quicker than the pot can feel the heat,
quicker than the fresh thorn withers,
the tempest shall carry them away.
And the just man shall be glad to see revenge,
he will wash his feet on the road in the blood of the unjust.
And a man will say, honesty has fruit:
there is a God who judges on earth.

God, save me from my enemies,
and put me out of reach of those who stand against me.
Rescue me from the unjust, save me from bloody and
    violent men,
because they have made an ambush against my life,
and the strong have gathered against me.
O God, I have not sinned, I have done no wrong.
They run to their positions but I give no offence:
rise and come to me and see.
O God, God of armies, God of Israel,
be aroused and handle all nations,
give no mercy to the treacherous and the unjust.
They run home at nightfall howling like dogs,
they go about in the city.
Their mouths are noisy and their lips are full of knives
because who hears?
God, you laugh at them,
you mock all nations.
My strength, my eyes are on you:
God is my castle.
The God that loves me will help me,
and God will make me look scornfully at all those who
    watch against me.
Do not kill them, my people will forget;
make them wanderers, bring them low, O God our shield.
The words between their lips are a sin in their mouth,
they shall be caught in their own pride
and in the curses and the lies of their speech.
Destroy them with anger, destroy them, make them
    nothing;

they shall know that God governs in Jacob
as far as the ends of the earth.
They run home at nightfall howling like dogs,
they go about the city.
They wander for food,
they growl until they are satisfied.
I will celebrate your strength with singing,
and shout for gladness in the morning because of your
    mercy,
because you have been my castle and my refuge in a day of
    troubles.
O my strength, I will praise you with the harp,
because God is my castle and my loving God.

God, you have rejected us and broken us down;
you have been angry, take us back now.
You have shaken the earth and split it open;
cure the gaps of the earth, because it trembles.
You have made your people see a terrible thing,
you gave us wine so that we staggered.
You have given a flag to those that fear you,
to fly it for truth.
Rescue your beloved ones,
save us with your hand, hear my prayer.
God has spoken in his holy place:
I will take pleasure:
I will distribute Shechem,
I will divide up the valley of Succoth,
Gilead is mine, Manasseh is mine,
Ephraim is my helmet, Judah is my sceptre,
Moab is my washpot, I throw down my shoe on Edom,
shout at me, Philistines.
Who will bring me into the fortified city?
Who will take me into Edom?
Is it not you, God, who rejected us
and will not go out with our armies, O God?
Help us in trouble,
human aid is an empty thing.
Through God we shall do mightily,
because he will tread down our enemies.

God, hear my cry, listen to my prayer.
I will cry out to you from the end of the earth in despair.
Put me on a high crag,
because you are my refuge
and my strong tower against all enemies.
I will live in your tent for ever,
I will shelter under cover of your wings.
God, you have heard my vows,
you have given an inheritance to those who fear your name.
Give days to the king's life,
let him live through generations,
let him sit for ever in the sight of God,
send mercy and faithfulness to guard him.
I will praise your name with the harp for ever,
I will pay you my promises day after day.

My soul is silent towards God alone,
my help comes from him.
He is my only rock and my salvation,
he is my castle, I shall not be shifted.
How long will you attack a man, all murderers together,
like a tottering wall, like a smashed fence?
They plan to drive me out of my stronghold,
they are pleased with their lies:
they bless in their mouths and they curse in their guts.
My soul, be silent towards God alone,
he is my hope.
He is my only crag and my salvation,
he is my castle, I shall not be shifted.
My salvation is with God, my honour is with God,
he is the crag of my strength and my refuge.
O people, trust him always; breathe out your hearts to him,
    God is our refuge.
The sons of man are an empty thing, they are illusions;
put them all together in the scales, their weight is emptiness.
Have no confidence in oppression and the emptiness of
    theft,
do not set your hearts on increases of wealth.
One thing God has said: two things I have heard:
strength is with God, and mercy is with you, O God,
because you pay every man his wages.

63

God, you are my God, I will look for you early;
my spirit has thirsted for you, my flesh has longed for you
in a desert which is weary and without water.
I have visited you in your holy place,
I have seen your strength and your glory.
Because your mercy is better than life,
my lips will praise you.
I will bless you during my life,
I will raise my hands in your name.
My spirit is full, it is filled with richness,
and my mouth is full of praises and shouts of gladness.
I have remembered you in my bed,
I have thought of you through the night-watches,
because you have been my help;
I will shout for joy in the shadows of your wings.
My spirit sticks to you, your right hand holds me tightly.
Those that hunt me for my life shall go down into the
depth of the earth.
They shall be handed over to the sword, they shall be the
belongings of jackals.
And the king will have joy in God,
whoever swears by him will be glad because of him,
because the mouths of liars will be stopped.

God, hear my voice complaining,
keep my life from the fear of enemies.
Hide me from the conspiracy of the wicked,
and the assembly of the unjust.
Their tongue is a sharp sword,
they shoot arrows of poisoned words
to strike the innocent man from an ambush;
they shoot suddenly and they fear nothing.
They take a grip on wickedness, they lay secret snares.
They say, Who will see us?
They make plans for injustice, they plot a clever plot,
their inner parts and all their thoughts are hidden.
The arrow of God strikes them,
they are suddenly wounded,
they stumble over their own tongues.
Everyone who sees them runs away, and all men are afraid,
they acknowledge the work of God and understand what
   he has done.
The just man will rejoice in God and shelter in him,
and all the good-hearted will speak gladly.

It is right to praise you, O God, in Zion,
and to perform promises,
because you answer prayer.
All flesh comes to you, O God.
Wickedness is heavy, we cannot handle it;
cover our sins.
What blessings a man has when you have chosen him and
bring him close;
he will live around your house.
We shall see the joy of the excellence of your house,
and the holy place of your temple.
You will answer us proceeding terribly and with justice,
O God of our freedom:
hope of all the ends of the earth
and the furthest people of the sea.
His strength establishes mountains,
his belt is power.
He makes the noises of the seas be silent,
the noises of waves and the roaring of peoples.
And the people of the furthest places are afraid
because of the signs you have made,
you shall make the gateway of morning and of evening to
shout with joy.
You have visited the earth and made it abundant,
you have made it very rich.
The river of God is full of water, you raise up corn.
This is your work on earth:
to water furrows, to break up ridges,
to soften with rain, to bless the growth.

You have crowned the year with goodness;
your feet drip riches,
they drip in the pastures of the desert,
and the mountains have a belt of gladness.
The fields are coated with sheep,
the valleys are coated with corn;
they will shout and they will sing.

Shout to God, all the earth.
Sing to the glory of his name with the harp.
Praise him gloriously.
Say to God, You proceed terribly:
your enemies cringe because of the greatness of your
    strength.
The whole earth shall bow to you,
it shall sing to you with the harp,
they shall praise your name with the harp.
Come and see what God has done,
he is terrible in his work on the sons of man.
He has made the sea dry land,
they walk through the river,
we shall be glad with him in that place.
His power governs for ever, and his eyes watch the peoples:
let the rebels not be proud.
Bless God, O you peoples, let his praise be heard.
Because he has established our souls alive,
and has not permitted our feet to stagger.
O God, you have proved us,
you have made us fine like the refining of silver.
You have brought us into a trap,
you have tied heaviness to our bodies,
you have put a man to ride on our heads.
We have walked through fire and through water,
you have brought us out into a generous place.
I will go to your house with sacrifices,
I will pay you my promises,
which I made in my distress, and which I spoke.

I will offer you the sacrifice of fat sheep
and the sweet smell of rams,
I will bring you bullocks and billy-goats.
Come and listen: I will say to all who fear God
what he has done for my spirit.
I spoke and called to him,
the words in my mouth were his praises.
If I have injustice in my heart God will not hear me.
Truly God has heard me: he has listened to my voice.
I bless God, because he has not turned away my prayer,
he has not turned away his mercy.

67

God be good to us and bless us
and make his face shine on us,
for his path to be known on the earth
and his salvation among all the peoples.
O God, the peoples will thank you.
The nations shall be glad and shout for joy;
you will judge the peoples with justice
and govern the nations on the earth.
O God, the nations will thank you,
all the nations will thank you.
The earth has given its harvest;
God shall bless us, he is our God.
God will bless us,
and all the ends of the earth will fear him.

68

God rises and his enemies are scattered:
those that hate him run away from him like smoke
    that vanishes,
like the melting of wax in the fire;
the unjust will be destroyed by God.
The just will be glad, they will rejoice because of God:
they will have great joy and gladness.
Sing to God, sing his name with the harp,
praise him who rides on the desert,
whose name is Who Is;
be glad because of him,
father of the fatherless, justice of widowed women,
God in his holy place.
God brings home the abandoned,
he brings out prisoners to a prosperous life,
only the rebellious remain in a barren country.
O God, when you led your people out,
when you travelled in the desert,
earth shook and heaven shivered in the presence of God,
God of Sinai, God of Israel.
O God, you have rained down goodness,
your country was weary and you refreshed it.
Your flock is there,
you have provided for the poor with goodness, O God.
God shall speak
and very many shall run away,
they shall run away and women at home shall distribute the
    loot.
You lay between the cattle-pens;
the wings of a dove are silvered over,

the feathers of a dove are yellow,
they shine with fine gold;
when God scatters the kings
snow falls on Zalmon.
The mountain of Bashan is a mountain of God,
it is a mountain of crests.
Crested mountains, why do you look with envy
at the mountain where God has delighted to be,
where God will live for ever?
The chariots of God are in tens of thousands,
and in many thousands.
God is in them,
the God of Sinai in his holy place.
You have gone up high, you have taken captives,
you have taken the tribute of men
who will not live with God: Who Is.
Blessed be God
who carries us day after day,
God of our freedom:
God, our God, who saves from death.
God breaks the heads of his enemies,
he breaks the scalp of the wrong-living man.
God has spoken:
I shall bring you from Bashan,
I shall bring you from the bottom of the sea,
to dip your feet in blood,
and your dogs to eat a dinner from your enemies.
O God, they see you come in,
my God and my king coming in his holy place:
singers in front, musicians behind,
and the girls with the timbrels are among them.
Bless God in your assemblies,
whose origin is in Israel, bless God.

Benjamin the youngest leads them,
the company of the lords of Judah,
the lords of Zebulun, the lords of Naphtali.
God has commanded your power;
O God, strengthen your work on us.
Because of your temple, which is in Jerusalem,
kings shall bring you gifts.
Strike at the beasts among the reeds,
the herd of wild bulls, the bull-calfs of nations,
that humble themselves for pieces of silver.
God scatters those peoples who delight in war.
Ambassadors will come from Egypt,
Ethiopians shall stretch out their hands to God.
Kingdoms of the earth, sing to God,
sing with the harp to God
who rides on the ancient heavens;
he shall speak with his voice, his voice is strong.
Praise the strength of God,
he is almighty over Israel, his power is in the sky.
O God, you are terrible from your holy place, God of
    Israel.
You give power and strength to your people:
bless God.

69

Save me, God, because the water is coming into my soul,
I am sinking in deep marshes, I am not able to stand,
I have got into a deep place in the water,
the flood is running above my head.
I am tired out with shouting, my throat is burnt,
my sight has failed searching for my God.
Those that hate me for no reason are more numerous than
 the hair on my head,
I have been treacherously cut down by strong enemies,
I have given back what I have never taken.
God, you know my foolishness, and my sins are not hidden
 from you.
Do not make those that trust you be ashamed because of
 me,
O God, the God of armies.
Do not make those that look to you be ashamed because of
 me,
God of Israel.
I have accepted an insult because of you,
my face has been covered with shame,
I have become a stranger to my brothers and a foreigner to
 my full brothers;
jealousy for your house has eaten me up
and whoever insults you has insulted me.
So I dressed in sackcloth,
I became something proverbial.
People at the town gates mumbled about me,
and the drinkers made a comic song about me.
As for me, O God, I pray to you,
O God, in a good hour.

God, in the multitude of your goodness answer me with
reliable salvation.
Save me from the marshes, let me not sink,
rescue me from my enemies and the deep water.
Make the flood not run over me,
make the deep place not drown me,
make my grave not shut its mouth on me.
Answer me, God, because of the goodness of your mercy,
come to me because of the number of your mercies.
Do not hide your face from your servant, O God,
because I am in trouble,
answer me quickly:
be with my spirit and rescue me.
You know my bad name and my shame and my dishonour,
you see my enemies.
Dishonour has broken my heart,
I am weak, I look for comfort, there is no one.
I look for a comforter and find no one.
They gave me wormwood,
when I was thirsty they gave me vinegar.
Trap them with their own table,
make it trip their friends.
Darken their eyes, take away their eyesight,
make their bodies stagger and stagger.
Be angry with them,
strike them with the indignation of your anger.
Their camp will be demolished
and no one will be left in their tents
because they have hunted down the man you struck,
and they have increased the suffering of the man you
wounded.
Add injustice to their injustice,
let them not enter into your justice.

Let them be blotted out of the book of life
and their names not be written among the just.
I am poor and suffering;
O God, your freedom will lift me high up,
I will sing and praise the name of God.
I will honour him and give him thanks,
and God will be pleased,
more than with a bull,
more than with a young bull and his horn and hoof.
Let the poor see this and be glad,
let those who look for God be refreshed:
God hears the destitute,
God does not despise his slaves.
Heaven and earth shall praise him,
and the sea and everything that moves in the sea.
God will save Zion
and build up the cities of Judah:
they shall live in them and inherit them,
and the children of his servants shall inherit,
and those who love his name shall live in them.

God save me, God be quick and protect me.

Those who want to murder me will be ashamed and con-
fused,

those who are pleased with my harm will be ashamed and
driven back,

those who shout Ha! Ha! will turn away and be ashamed.

Everyone who looks for God will be joyful and glad be-
cause of him,

they will say continually, God is great,

everyone whose confidence is in your help.

I am poor and destitute;

O God come quickly.

You are my help and my freedom;

O God do not be long.

O God, I have taken refuge in you;
do not shame me for ever.
Be just, rescue me, set me free:
listen to me and save me.
Be a castle of refuge on a rock to me, commander of my
  salvation:
you are my crag among rocks, you are my strong place.
O God, save me from the hands of the wicked,
from the unjust and the cruel man:
because, O God, you are my hope,
I have trusted you from my first youth.
I leaned on you in the womb,
you brought me out from my mother's body.
I will praise you always.
Many have been amazed at me,
you have been my refuge and my strength.
My mouth is full of your praise and your glory the whole
  day.
Do not abandon me when I am old,
do not leave me when my strength is finished.
My enemies have spoken against me,
those who watch against my life have plotted together.
They say, God has left him,
hunt him and take him, because there is no one to save him.
God be close to me,
O my God come quickly to help me.
The enemies of my life will be shamed, they will come to
  nothing,
those that seek my harm will be overwhelmed with
  rebukes and dishonour.

I will hope continually,

I will add praises to your praise.

I will express your justice and your protection the whole
day.

I cannot measure it:

I will proceed by the power of my God,

I will speak of your justice and of no other.

O God you have instructed me from my youth until now,

I will speak about your wonderful work.

O God do not leave me in my old age and white hair,

I will tell your power to a new generation,

I will tell your strength to all future time.

O God your justice is the absolute of height,

you have done very great things;

O God, who is like you?

You have made me suffer many and dreadful troubles,

you will turn and save my life,

you will turn back and bring me up out of the depths of the
earth.

You will make me very great, you will turn to comfort me.

And I will thank you with the music of the lyre

for your faithfulness, O God.

I will praise you singing with the harp,

holy one of Israel.

My lips will shout with gladness when I sing to you with
the harp,

and my soul which you have saved will shout with gladness.

And my tongue will speak of your justice the whole day,

because those who seek my harm have been ashamed and
frustrated.

O God give the King your judgement,
and the King's son your uprightness.
He will judge your people uprightly
and the poor with judgement.
The mountains shall bring peace to the people,
the hills shall bring them justice.
He will be the judge of the poor among the people,
he will save the sons of the destitute man,
he will crush the oppressive man.
They shall fear you under the sun and under the moon
for generations of generations.
He shall drop like the rain on clear ground,
and like the shower of a dewfall on the earth,
and the upright man will flourish in his days
in a great peace, until there is no more moon.
He shall govern from sea to sea,
from the river to the ends of the earth.
The people of the desert will bow to him
and his enemies will eat dust.
The kings of Tarshish and the islands will bring presents,
the kings of Sheba and Seba will come with tribute,
every king will bow to him
and every nation will serve him.
He will save the poor man when he cries out,
and the destitute man and the man no one helps.
He will pity the destitute and the poor man
and protect the lives of the poor.
He will save their lives from violence and oppression,
their blood will be precious to him.

He shall live, they will give him gold from Sheba
and pray for him continually:
they will bless him the whole day.
The corn will be thick in the earth,
it will climb over the crests of the mountains
like the fruits of Lebanon,
and the city will flourish like grass over the ground.
His name will live for ever,
his name will breed under the sun,
they will bless themselves by him,
every nation will bless him.
Bless God, the God of Israel,
the only worker of wonders.
Bless his glorious name for ever.
May the whole earth be full of his glory.
Amen and amen.

God is good to Israel, to the clean-hearted.
I nearly turned away,
I all but stumbled,
because I was envious of boasters and I saw the peace of the
  wicked.
They are not hanged,
they are strong and healthy.
They are outside the sufferings of mankind,
they are not whipped like other men.
They wear pride like a gold chain,
they are dressed in violence.
Their eyes peer out through fatness,
the fantasy of their hearts is riotous.
They mock, they speak maliciously of oppression,
they talk from a height.
Their mouths are as high as heaven
and their tongues wander round the earth:
Let the people gather here,
they shall have cold water.
And they say, How does God know?
Is there knowledge in heaven?
These are unjust,
and the rich in this time have increased their wealth.
It is a folly I have cleaned my heart
and washed my hands in innocence.
I have been lashed all day,
I have been insulted every morning.
And if I said, I will say the same,
I would betray all your children.
And I puzzled to understand this,

and it was painful to me,
until I went to the holy place of God;
and I will think of their final end.
You have put them onto slippery ground,
you have made them a ruin:
they collapsed in a moment of time,
they are finished and destroyed with terrors.
Like a dream to a man awake,
O God, when you wake you will despise them like a fantasy.
My heart was sour and my balls ached,
I was stupid and understood nothing,
I was an animal in your presence.
I am with you always,
you have taken hold of my hand.
You will lead me with your wisdom
and bring me into honour.
Who is there for me in heaven?
With you I have no other delight on earth.
My heart has withered and my flesh has withered;
God is the rock-refuge of my heart, and my inheritance for
    ever.
Because away from God they will perish,
he has destroyed those who go elsewhere and fornicate.
But my good is to be close to God,
my refuge is in my God,
and to speak of what he has done.

III

O God, why do you disown for ever?

In the smoke of your anger against the sheep of your
    pastures.

Remember your people, your possession for ages,

you picked it like your stick;

this is mount Zion, you have lived in it.

Turn your steps to the ruins of ages,

the enemy has devastated everything in the holy place.

Enemies have howled in your meeting place,

they have put up signs of triumph.

They were like axemen in the thickets of the woods,

they smashed the cut stone with hand-axes and hammers,

they attacked your holy place with fire,

they demolished the home of your name.

They said, We shall ruin them all together.

They have burnt every meeting-place of God on earth.

We have no flag, we have no prophet,

we have no one who knows how long.

O God, how long shall the enemy insult you?

Will he mock your name for ever?

Why do you hold back your hand?

Why is your right hand on your chest?

God is my king from ages,

he sets free on earth.

You have broken open the sea with strength

and crushed the heads of the monsters in the sea.

You have cracked the head of Leviathan

and given him to the people of the desert for their food.

You have broken open a spring and a stream,

you have dried perpetual rivers.

The day is yours and the night is yours,
you made the moon and the sun,
you set up all the limits of the earth,
and created summer and winter.
God remember that your enemy has insulted you
and a foolish people has mocked your name.
Do not leave the life of your wood-dove to wild animals;
you will not abandon the lives of the poor for ever.
Remember the promise,
because the dark places and the pastures have been full of
    violence.
Never let the victims be ashamed and turn away;
the destitute and the poor man will praise your name.
Stand, God, and make your case;
remember the insults of idiots all day long.
Do not forget the voices of your enemies,
the endless noise of those who stand against you.

We thank you, O God, we thank you.
Your name is with us,
your marvellous works declare it.
When I shall set a time
I shall judge in justice.
The earth crumbles with everyone that lives on it,
but I have built columns for it.
I said to the proud, Do not boast;
and to the unjust, Do not toss your heads;
do not lift your horns and your head against heaven
or utter in the arrogance of your neck.
There is nothing in the east and nothing in the west
and nothing in the desert or the mountains,
there is only God who judges,
he puts down and he raises up.
There is a cup in the hand of God
and the wine is foaming, it is full of a mixture;
he has poured it, all the unjust on earth shall drink it,
to the sediment and the last drop.
And I will praise him for ever,
I will sing to the God of Jacob with a harp.
I shall break the horns on the heads of the unjust,
and the head of the just man and his horns will be lifted up.

God is known in Judah, his name is great in Israel,
his tent has been in Salem and his home was in Zion.
He has broken up the arrows that were like lightning,
and the shield and sword and the arms of war.
You are ablaze and terrible
coming down from the bad mountains,
the bodies of the brave have been robbed,
they sleep their sleep,
the strongest of men cannot move their hands.
O God of Jacob, at your stroke
the horse sleeps and the chariot sleeps.
You are terrifying:
who can stand up to you in your anger?
You have made judgement heard from heaven,
earth was afraid and was quiet,
when you stood up to judge, O God,
to save the humiliated on the earth.
You will confront the anger of mankind and they shall
    know you,
you will wear the extremes of anger like a belt.
Make vows to God and pay them to your God,
all people around him shall pay him their gift because he
    is terrible,
he will strike at the spirits of princes,
he is very terrible to the kings of the earth.

My voice will cry out to God,
I will cry out to God; he has heard me.
I looked for God on the day of my trouble,
I lifted my hand in the night without tiring,
my spirit would not be comforted.
When I remember God, I groan;
when I consider, my spirit is weak.
You have pulled my eyes open,
I am disturbed, I have nothing to say.
I considered past time and the ages of years.
I will think of music in the night,
I will consider in my heart, I will search my spirit:
Does God abandon for ever?
Will he never be kind?
Is his goodness over for ever?
Has his promise to generations come to an end?
Has God forgotten mercy?
Has he stopped up his love with anger?
And I said, My distress is this,
the years of the hand of God.
I will remember the work of God
and his wonders through the ages.
I will remember what you have done,
I will consider your work.
O God, you proceed in your holy place;
what god is as great as God?
You are the wonder-working God,
you have shown your strength to the peoples.
You have rescued your people with the power of your arm,
the sons of Jacob, the sons of Joseph.

O God, the sea has seen you,
the sea has seen you and it suffered,
and the deep places were disturbed.
The multitude of the clouds dropped their water,
heaven uttered,
the arrows of God are flying.
The thunder of the voice of God is in the tempest,
the lightnings have lighted up the world.
The earth is afraid and it shivers,
you are walking in the sea,
you are moving in the multitude of the water,
you have not left a footprint,
you have guided your people like sheep,
by the hands of Moses and of Aaron.

My people, listen to my law,
hear what I say.
I will tell a story,
I will speak in old sayings.
We know them, they are familiar,
we have heard them from our fathers.
We shall not keep them secret from our children,
we shall tell the new generation the praises of God,
his power, and the wonders of his work.
He has created a witness in Jacob
and a law in Israel,
which he commanded our fathers to teach to their children,
for the new generation to know it
and for sons to be born and to teach it to their sons,
to put their trust in God
and not to forget the work of God,
and to defend his commandments.
They shall not be like their fathers,
a resisting and rebellious generation
whose heart was not fixed, nor was their spirit resolute with
    God.
The sons of Ephraim were archers, they shot with bows,
but they turned and ran on the day of battle.
They neglected the promise of God,
they determined not to move by the law of God,
they forgot his work
and the wonderful things he had shown them.
He worked a miracle for their fathers in Egypt
in the place called Zoan,

he broke open the sea and made them walk through it,
he made the water stand up in a heap.
He guided them with a cloud all day,
with the light of a fire all night.
He broke open rocks in the desert,
he made them drink deep water.
He brought out running water from the crags of rocks,
he set loose a river of water.
They sinned again,
they rebelled against God in the desert,
they tempted God in their heart
with their desire and demanding food.
And they spoke against him and said,
Can God make a dinner in the desert?
He struck the rock and water flowed and the stream was
    running over.
Can he give us bread as well?
Will he give his people meat?
And God was angry,
he lit a fire against Jacob, he was angry with Israel,
because they had not believed in God,
they had not trusted his salvation.
And he commanded the sky above them and opened the
    doors of heaven.
He dropped a rain of manna and gave them the bread of
    heaven,
and man ate the bread of the strong ones,
he provided and he filled them.
Then he set loose the east wind in heaven,
and by his power he commanded the south wind,
and he rained a dust of meat,
birds like the sand of the sea;

he dropped them in his camp
and around the place he lived in.
They ate and they were very full
and their desire was satisfied.
But they went on craving with the food still in their
    mouths,
and God was angry with them,
and he killed the strong men,
he destroyed the youth of Israel.
And in this they sinned again,
they disbelieved his miracles.
He diminished the days of their life to one breath,
and the years of their life to one gasp.
And when he murdered them they looked to him,
they turned to God, they looked for God.
They remembered that God was their mountain,
that God in heaven saved them.
They deceived him with words, they told him lies,
their heart was not right,
they were not true to his promise.
But God is merciful, he purifies sin, not destroys it;
he called back his anger, he would not quite be furious.
He considered that they were flesh and bone,
a breath that blows and vanishes.
They resisted him very often in the desert,
they grieved him in the wilderness.
They tested God,
they grieved the holy one of Israel,
not remembering his hands
or the day he saved them from the enemy,
who did miracles in Egypt
and wonders in the place called Zoan.
He turned the rivers to blood,

he made the running water undrinkable,
he sent swarms of flies to eat them and frogs to ruin them,
he increased caterpillars and blessed the work of the locusts,
he murdered the vines with hail and the mulberries with
  frost,
and the cattle with the fire of lightning.
He threw down the heat of his fury:
in rage and indignation and trouble and bad angels.
He cleared a path for anger,
he let their souls die, he left their lives to the plague,
he struck every firstborn son in Egypt,
the principal strength in the tents of Ham.
He guided his people like sheep,
he took them like a flock through the desert,
he brought them safely, they were not afraid.
The sea drowned their enemies.
He took them into the country of his holy place
and the mountain which is in his hand.
He pushed out nations and measured their inheritance,
and brought the tribes of Israel into their tents.
And they resisted and tempted the most high God,
they refused his proof,
they betrayed him like their fathers,
they twisted like a bad bow,
they angered him with hill-shrines,
their carved gods made him jealous.
God heard them, he was enraged, he utterly abandoned
  Israel.
He left his house at Shiloh and his tent among men.
He gave his power to captivity
and his honour to the hands of his enemies.
He handed over his people to a sword,
he was angry with his possession.

The young men died by fire,
the young girls were not married,
the priests died by the knife
and the widows did no weeping.
And God woke as if from sleep, like a strong man shouting
    with joy in his wine,
he struck his enemies backwards, he insulted them for ever.
He deserted the tent of Joseph, nor did he choose the tribe
    of Ephraim,
but he chose the tribe of Judah and the mountain of Zion,
    and he loved it.
He built his holy place high, he based it like the earth for
    ever.
He picked out David his servant and took him from the
    sheepfolds.
He took him from the ewes in lamb
for the shepherd of Jacob his people and Israel his possession.
And he fed them with a simple heart,
and guided them with the cunning of his hands.

God, the nations have entered your possession,
they have dirtied the place of your holiness,
they have made Jerusalem a pile of stones.
They have given the dead bodies of your servants to the
    birds
and the flesh of your holy ones to the animals.
They have spilt blood like water around Jerusalem.
There is no one left to bury the dead,
we are an insult with our neighbours,
a mockery and a despised thing to everyone near us.
O God, how long? Will you be angry for ever?
Is your jealousy a fire?
Use your anger on the nations that have never known you
and the kingdoms that have never cried out to you.
They have devoured Jacob,
they have devastated the place he lived in.
Forget the wickedness of our fathers,
make your goodness come to us quickly,
because we have been brought very low.
God of our freedom, help us for the honour of your name,
    and save us.
Why should the nations say, Where is there God?
Let us see them pay for the spilt blood of your servants.
Listen to the groaning of prisoners.
Rescue the condemned to death, make your arm strong.
God, pay back our neighbours seven times in their laps
for the mockeries they mocked you with.
And we your people, the sheep you take to pasture, will
    thank you for ever
and praise you in every generation.

Shepherd of Israel,
listen to us;
who guides Joseph like a flock,
who sits on the wings of spirits,
shine on us;
for Ephraim and Benjamin and Manasseh,
wake and be powerful and come and save us.
O God bring us back and make your face shine on us
and we shall be saved.
O God, the God of armies,
how long will you smoulder on against the prayers of your
    people?
You have fed them with the bread of tears,
and given them a drink of very many tears.
You have set our neighbours quarrelling over us,
our enemies mock among themselves;
O God of armies, bring us back and make your face shine
    on us
and we shall be saved.
You brought a vine from Egypt,
you drove out nations and planted it,
you cleared ground and the root of the vine rooted
and it covered the ground,
and the shadows of the vine spread over mountains,
and the branches were like the cedars of God,
and the shoots of the vine extended to the sea,
and the young stems to the great river.
Why have you broken down the wall around it?
and everyone who passes picks,
and the wild boars of the forest savage it,

and animals out of the fields feed on it.
O God of armies,
turn back, look down from heaven and see,
visit this vine:
the growth you planted with your hands,
the son you brought up strong.
They have cut it down and burnt it;
let them perish by the anger of your face.
Put out your hand to the man who is the work of your
  hand:
to the son of man you brought up strong.
We shall not turn away from you,
you shall keep us alive and we shall proclaim your name.
God, the God of armies, bring us back and make your face
  shine on us
and we shall be saved.

Shout for joy to God our strength,
shout to the God of Jacob.
Come with music
and the timbrel and the pleasant harp and the lyre.
Sound the horn of newness
at the full moon on the solemn day,
because it is a law in Israel,
a command of the God of Jacob.
He gave it to Joseph to keep
when he went across Egypt.
I shall hear the voice of a mouth I never knew.
I have taken off the load from his shoulders
and his hands have let go of the basket.
You cried out in trouble and I saved you,
I have answered you hidden in thunder,
and tested you at the river of quarrels.
Listen, my people,
I will witness against you, Israel,
if you will hear me.
There shall be no foreign god among you,
and you shall not worship any foreign god.
I am God your God
who brought you out of Egypt;
open your mouth and I will fill it.
But my people did not listen to my voice,
and Israel did not want me,
and I dismissed them in their stubbornness
to follow their own mind.
O, if my people would hear me,
and Israel would go by my path,

I will put down their enemies in a moment,
I will move my hand against them,
and those that hate God shall cringe to him,
and this time will last for ever.
I will feed them with the richest wheat.
I will fill them up with honey from the rocks.

God stands in the assembly of gods
to judge among gods.
How long will you judge unjustly?
and favour the persons of the wicked?
Be judges of the weak and the fatherless,
give justice to the destitute and very poor.
Rescue the weak and poor man,
set him free from the action of the unjust.
They neither know nor understand this,
they proceed in darkness,
and the base of the earth is shifted:
I said, You are gods,
you are all sons of the most high God,
and you shall die like mankind,
you shall fall down and die like all princes.
O God, stand and judge the earth,
because all the nations in the world shall be your possession.

God, do not rest,
God, do not be quiet, God, do not be silent:
because your enemies are raging,
and those that hate you are lifting up their heads.
They are plotting cunningly against your people,
they are making plans against your protected ones.
They say, Come, we shall destroy them as a nation,
and the name of Israel will be forgotten.
They have discussed it and agreed on it,
they will make an alliance against you:
the tents of Edom and the Ishmaelites,
Moab and the Hagarenes, Gebal and Ammon and Amalek,
and Philistia and the people of Tyre,
the Assyrians are with them,
and they will fight for the children of Lot.
Treat them like Midian at En Harod,
like Sisera, like Jabin at the river Kishon,
who were slaughtered and lay like dung on the ground.
Treat their princes like Oreb and Zeeb,
and all their chief men like Zebah and Zalmunna.
They said, We shall take possession of the territories of God.
O my God, blast them like dust in the desert
and like chaff in the wind:
like a fire burning down a forest,
like the flames on a mountainside,
strike them in the tempest, overwhelm them in the whirling
    of wind.
Put shame into their faces,
make them look for your name, O God.

They shall be ashamed and confused for ever,
and ruined, and they shall perish.
O God, they shall know that your name alone
is most high over the whole earth.

84

I have loved your tents,
O God of armies.
My spirit has withered, it has longed for the courtyards of
    God;
my heart and my flesh have shouted for gladness to the
    living God.
The sparrow has found a house
and the swallow has made a nest for her young –
your altars, God of armies,
my king and my God.
Happy are those who have lived in your house;
they shall praise you always.
Happy is the man whose strength is in God,
and the roads of pilgrimage are in his heart.
They shall pass through the valley of weeping
and make it a spring of water;
the early rain will cover it in blessings.
They shall move from fortress to fortress,
and appear before God in Zion.
O God, the God of armies, hear my prayer,
O God of Jacob, listen.
God our shield, regard us,
look into the face of your Anointed one.
Because a day in your courtyards is better than a thousand
    days,
and I have chosen to remain in the porch of the house of my
    God
and not to live in the tents of the wicked;
because God who is God is a sun and a shield,

God gives goodness and glory,
he will not refuse good things to the innocent.
O God of armies,
happy is the man who trusts you.

85

O God, you have been good to your country
and turned back the turning away of Jacob.
You have taken away wickedness from the people and
  covered up their sins.
You have called back your anger,
and put aside the hotness of rage.
Turn us back, God of our freedom,
and leave off your displeasure.
Will you be angry with us for ever?
Will you drag out your anger through generations?
Will you not rather change and make us live?
And your people will be glad because of you.
God, let us see your goodness,
and give us your protection.
I will hear what God says,
he will wish Peace to his people and his saints,
who have turned to him in their hearts.
His protection is very close to those who fear him,
his honour is in our country.
Good and true have come together,
right and peace have kissed,
truth has sprung up out of the earth,
and right has looked down from heaven;
and God shall be good
and the earth give its fruit,
and right will walk ahead of him
and make a road for his feet.

86

O God listen and answer me,
because I am destitute and very poor;
keep my spirit because I am holy;
save your servant, O my God, because he has trusted you.
Be good to me, God, because I will call to you all day.
God make the spirit of your servant glad,
because you are good and forgiving, O God,
and very merciful to everyone that cries out to you.
O God listen to my prayer and hear me in my petitions.
I will cry out to you on my day of trouble
because you will answer me.
O God, there is no one like you among the gods,
and no other work is like your work.
All the nations that you made will come to you and wor-
    ship, O God,
they will honour your name,
because you are great and your work is wonders,
and you alone are God.
God, teach me your road,
I will walk by your faith;
make my heart fear your name.
O God my God, I will thank you with my whole heart,
I will glorify your name for ever,
because you are very good to me
and you have saved my spirit from the bottom of hell.
O God, the proud stood up against me,
and a tyrannous assembly hunted me for my life;
you were not in their sight.
O God, you are a God of mercy and goodness,
slow to be angry, and very merciful and faithful.

Turn to me and be good to me,
give your strength to your slave;
save me, I was born your slave.
Give me a good sign
and my enemies will be shamed,
because you have helped me and befriended me, O God.

His foundations are on the mountains of his holiness;
God loves the gates of Zion better than all the camps of
   Jacob.
Glorious things are said of you,
O city of God.
I will speak of Egypt and Babylon with my friends,
and of Philistia and Tyre and Ethiopia:
that such a man was born there.
But it will be said to Zion,
man and man were born in her,
and the most high God shall make her strong.
When God numbers the peoples he shall write
that such a man was born in her.
There shall be singers, there shall be dancers:
All my springs are in her.

O God, the God of my freedom,
I have cried out to you day and night.
Let my prayer reach you, listen to my call,
because my spirit is filled up with bad things
and my life has gone close to hell.
I was counted with those who go down into the earth,
I had no strength.
I was one of the dead
and the murdered men who lie down in their graves,
who have dropped out of your memory
and fallen away from your hand.
You have set me down in the lowest part of the earth
and in the bottom of darkness.
Your indignation has been heavy on me,
you have overwhelmed me with the whole sea.
You have taken my friends far away from me
and made me a horror to them;
I am shut in, I shall not come out.
My eyes have faded away with sorrow;
O God, I have cried out to you every day,
I have spread out my hands to you.
Will you do miracles for the dead?
Will the dead stand up and praise you?
Will they celebrate your goodness in their graves?
And your constancy in their nothingness?
Will they know your miracles in the dark?
And your justice in the country of forgetting?
O God, I have cried out to you
and my prayer shall come to you in the morning.

O God, why have you deserted my spirit,
why do you hide your face from me?
I was destitute and dying from my youth,
I have suffered your terrors and I shall go mad.
Your fire has gone over me,
your terrors have destroyed me.
I drown in them like water the whole day,
they have closed in together.
You have taken away my lovers and my friends,
my conversation is with darkness.

I will sing of the goodness of God always,
my voice will tell his faithfulness to generations.
I said, Goodness will stand for ever,
and his faithfulness will be fixed in the heavens.
I have made an agreement with my chosen,
I have sworn an oath to David my servant,
I will strengthen your seed for ever
and make your throne stand for generations.
O God, the heavens celebrate your wonders,
your faithfulness in the assembly of the holy:
who can be compared to God in heaven,
who is like him among the sons of God?
God is very terrible in the gathering of the holy,
he is fearful and above all of them.
O God, the God of armies, who is like you?
God, you are strong, and your faithfulness is round you.
You have mastered the pride of the sea
and quieted the tumult of the waves.
You have crushed Egypt like a wounded beast
and scattered your enemies with the strength of your arm.
Heaven is yours and the earth is yours,
the world and its fullness which you created.
You made the north and the south,
Tabor and Hermon shout with joy at your name.
Your arm is strong, your hand is mighty, your right hand
   is lifted up.
Your throne stands on right and on judgement,
your presence is goodness and faithfulness.
I bless the people that will shout with joy:

O God, they will walk by the light of your face,
they will be glad because of your name the whole day,
they will be lifted up because of your justice,
because you are their glorious strength,
by your goodwill our heads are lifted up.
Because God is our shield,
the holy one of Israel is our king.
You have spoken through a vision to your prophets,
you said, I have put power on a hero,
I have lifted up a man chosen from the people;
I have found David my servant,
I have anointed him with the oil of my holiness;
my hand will be fixed on him
and my arm will make him strong.
The enemy shall not trample on him
and the sons of wickedness shall not hurt him.
I will beat down his enemies in his sight,
I will strike those that hate him.
I will be faithful and good to him,
he will lift up his head because of my name.
I will put his hand into the sea
and his right hand into the rivers.
He shall cry out to me, You are my father,
and my God, and the crag of my freedom.
I shall make him my first son,
and very high over the kings of the earth.
I shall be good to him for ever,
my agreement will be firm with him.
I will strengthen his seed for ever
and his throne for the ages of heaven.
If his sons abandon my law and will not go by my judge-
    ment,
if they corrupt my laws and abandon my commandments,

I shall punish their sins with the stick
and whip them for their injustices.
I will not abolish my goodness to him,
I will not go back on my faith,
I will not spoil my agreement,
I will not change what my lips have spoken.
I have sworn one oath by my holiness;
I shall not lie to David;
his seed will be everlasting
and his throne like the sun in my sight;
it will last like the moon for ever,
which is a constant witness in heaven.
But now you have rejected him and left him,
you have been angry with your anointed and dirtied his
    crown on the earth,
you have battered down his walls and left his fortresses in
    ruins;
everyone that passed by took loot from him,
he was an insult among his neighbours.
You have lifted the right hands of those who came against
    him,
and made all his enemies glad.
You have turned aside the edge of his sword and broken his
    stand in battle.
You have stopped his bright shining and overturned his
    throne on the earth,
and diminished the time of his youth, and dressed him in
    shame.
How long, O God?
Will you hide for ever?
Is your anger a smouldering fire?
Think what is my lifetime,
what an empty thing you created in the children of men:

what man can live and never die?
Will he save his soul from the hands of hell?
O God, where is your first goodness?
You swore an oath to David in faith,
O God, remember the insulting of your servants,
I carry in my heart the mockeries of nations
and the bad words of your enemies, O God,
insulting in the steps of your anointed.
Bless God for ever. Amen and amen.

God, you have been our home
in every generation.
Before the mountains were born,
before the earth and the world burst out:
from everlasting to everlasting you are God.
You have crumbled mankind to dust
and said, Come back, children of man.
Because a thousand years are like yesterday in your sight,
and like an hour in the night-time:
you overwhelm them and they sleep,
in the morning they spring up like grass
that shoots up and flowers in the morning
and at evening it is cut down and it withers.
We have been destroyed by your anger,
and your fury has made us a chaos.
You have brought our wickedness into your sight
and our private sins into the light of your eyes.
All our days have been used up in your anger,
we have passed our years like a muttering.
Our lifetime is seventy years
and, if we are strong, then eighty years,
and the pride of those years is painfulness and emptiness,
they are over quickly and we are gone.
Who understands the power of your anger?
Your fury is like your fearfulness.
Teach us to measure a lifetime
and our hearts will be wise.
O God, come back: how long?
Think again about your servants.

Gladden us with your goodness in the morning,
and we shall shout with joy,
we shall be very glad all our days.
Gladden us over years as you humbled us in the years when
we suffered.
Let your servants see your work,
and your great glory in their children,
and the gentleness of God our God be on our heads.
Make our work stand:
O God, make our work stand.

Whoever hides with God
shall be under the shadows of the almighty.
I will say to God, my refuge and my tower,
my God, and I will trust him.
He will set you free from the bird-snare
and the overwhelming plague.
His feathers will cover you over,
you will creep away under his wings:
his loyalty is a shield and a protection.
You will not be afraid of any terror in the night,
or the arrow that flies by daylight,
or the plague that walks in darkness
or the fever that wastes at midday.
A thousand men will die beside you
and ten thousand on your right hand,
but it will not come near you.
But you will see with your own eyes
the wages of wickedness.
Because you have made God your refuge
and put your home in the most high.
No evil shall happen to you,
and the plague will not come to your tent.
He shall command his angels for you
to guard you wherever you move.
They shall lift you up in their hands,
you shall not hit your foot on a stone.
You shall walk on the jackal and the serpent,
you shall tread on the young lion and the dragon.
Because he clung to me I will save him,
I will lift him to a high place, because he knows my name.

He shall cry out to me and I will answer,
I am with him in his trouble.
I will set him free and make him glorious,
I will make him happy in the length of his time,
I will show him that God saves.

It is good to thank God
and sing praises of the name of the most high with the harp,
to declare his goodness in the morning,
and his faithfulness in the night:
with the ten strings and the lyre and the noises of the harp,
because, O God, I am glad of what you have done,
I will shout with joy at your work.
O God, you have worked mightily
and your thoughts have been very deep.
The man who is a brute will not know,
and the fool will not understand.
The wicked flourished like grass
and every unjust man was in flower,
and they shall be destroyed for ever.
And you are in the heights for ever, O God,
and look: O God, your enemies;
look: your enemies shall be wiped out,
those who do wickedly shall be scattered.
You have lifted up my head like the horns of a wild ox,
I am smothered in fresh oil.
My eyes have scorned those who watched against me,
and my ears have heard of the unjust who came against me.
The just man will flourish like the palm tree,
he will grow up like a cedar tree in Lebanon.
They have been planted in the house of God,
they will flourish in his courtyards;
they will still be growing in their old age,
they will be rich and fresh;
to show that God is honest,
he is my mountain,
there is nothing false in him.

93

God is king; he has dressed in majesty;
God has dressed in power; he has put on his belt;
and the world shall stand, it shall not shift.
Your throne stands from that time; you are ancient.
The voices of the rivers, O God,
the voices of the rivers have risen;
the rivers are roaring.
Above the voices of many mighty waters, the waves of the
    sea,
God in his height is most mighty.
Your promises are absolute;
O God, holiness belongs to your house
for everlasting.

God of revenge, O God the God of revenge,
appear.
Rouse yourself up, judge of the earth,
pay the proud their wages.
How long, O God,
how long will the wicked be happy?
And talk and be insolent?
And all the unjust boast?
O God, they crush your people,
they torture what belongs to you,
they murder widows and strangers,
they massacre the fatherless.
They say, God will not see,
the God of Jacob will not think about it.
Understand, you brutes;
you fools, when will you understand?
Shall God who created ears not hear?
Shall God who created eyes not see?
Shall God who punishes nations not strike?
God gives knowledge to man,
and he knows the thoughts of man,
and what a nothing they are.
O God, I bless the man you warn,
and teach him from your law,
to give him peace in the bad days
until the ditch is dug for the wicked.
God will not desert his people
and abandon his possession.
There will be justice of judgement,
and everyone with right in his heart will follow it.

Who will stand up with me against the wicked?
Who will be with me against the unjust?
If God had not helped me
my soul would soon have been in the land of silence.
When I say, My foot has tripped,
O God your goodness holds me up.
In the many, many thoughts I have
your consolation is the pleasure of my soul.
What have you to do with the destroying throne
that creates afflictions out of law?
But God is my high place,
and my God is the crag of my refuge.
He will turn back their injustice against them
and destroy them by their own badness;
God who is our God will destroy them.

Come and cry out with joy to God,
shout to the mountain of our freedom.
Come into his sight with praise,
cry out to him with music.
God is a great God,
he is a great king over all the gods.
The bottom of the earth is in his hand,
the tops of mountains are his.
The sea is his, he made it,
and his hands built the dry earth.
Come and bow down and worship,
we will kneel to God who made us.
Because he is our God, and we are the people of his flock,
we are his sheep.
Listen to his voice today.
Do not harden your hearts;
you did that at the Quarrel
and on the day of the Test in the desert.
Your fathers tried me and proved me, and they saw my
    work.
For forty years I loathed their generation;
I said, they are an unsteady people,
they do not know my paths.
Therefore I swore in my anger,
They shall not come into my peace.

Sing a new song to God;
sing to God all the earth;
sing to God and bless his name;
and proclaim every day that God saves.
Tell his glory to the nations
and his wonderful work to all the peoples.
God is great,
his praise is very great.
Be more afraid of him than of all the gods,
because all the gods of the nations are tiny gods,
and God created heaven.
He is glorious and royal,
there is power and glorious shining in his holy place.
O you families of peoples, give the honour to God,
give the honour of glory and of power to God;
give God the glory of his name;
bring offerings and come into the courtyards of his house.
Bow down to God and the majesty of his holiness,
let the whole earth shiver in his sight.
Say to the nations, God is king,
and the world shall stand, it shall not shift;
and he shall judge the peoples uprightly.
The heavens shall be glad and the earth shall rejoice,
and the sea and the creatures of the sea shall roar aloud.
The fields and the creatures of the fields shall be merry,
and all the trees of the woods shout with joy
in the sight of God because he has come,
because he has come to be judge of the earth:
he shall judge the world in justice
and the peoples in his faithfulness.

God is king, let the earth rejoice;
the islands of the sea are very many, they shall be glad.
Cloud and mist circle round him,
right and judgement are the foundation of his throne.
Fire goes ahead of him,
consuming his enemies around him.
His lightning has lighted up the world,
and the earth has seen it and shivered.
The mountains have melted like wax in the sight of God,
the God of the whole earth.
The heavens have declared his justice
and all peoples have seen his glory.
All the servants of statues shall be ashamed,
who boast about their little gods:
bow down to God all gods.
Zion heard and rejoiced,
and the daughters of Judah were glad
because of your judgements, O God.
Because you are most high above the whole earth
and very high above all the gods.
Faithful of God, hate evil:
God guards the spirits of his saints
and saves them from the hands of the unjust.
The seeds of light are sown for the just man
and the seeds of joy for the honest.
O you just, be glad in God
and thank him for the remembrance of his holiness.

Sing a new song to God,
because he has worked wonderfully.
His right hand and the arm of his holiness have saved.
God has shown that he saves,
he has made his justice known in the sight of nations.
He has remembered his goodness
and his faith to the house of Israel;
and all the ends of the earth have seen the protection of our
   God.
Shout to God, the whole earth,
break out and shout with joy,
sing praises with instruments of music.
Sing to God and praise him with the harp,
with harps and the music of voices
and the trumpet and the noise of the horn.
Shout in the sight of God who is the king.
The sea and the creatures of the sea shall roar aloud,
and the world and all the creatures of the world.
The rivers shall clap their hands
and the mountains shall exult together in the sight of God,
because he has come to judge the earth:
he shall judge the world in justice
and the peoples in right.

God is king and the peoples shall tremble,
he sits on the spirits of the air and the earth shall quake,
God is great in Zion and high above all nations.
They shall praise your name, the great and the terrible,
because it is holy,
and the king and his power because he has loved right.
You have established honesty
and created justice and right in Jacob.
Praise God who is our God,
and worship at his footstool
because he is holy.
Moses and Aaron were his priests, and Samuel called out his
    name;
they called to God and he answered them;
he spoke to them in the pillar of cloud,
and they kept his commandments and the law that he gave
    them.
O God our God, you answered them,
you were a forgiving God to them
and the avenger of what was done to them.
Praise God who is our God
and worship at his holy mountain,
because God is holy.

100

Shout to God all the earth,
serve God with rejoicing,
come to him with shouting and gladness.
Know that God is God,
he made us, we are his,
his people and the sheep of his flock.
Enter his gates with thanksgiving
and his courts with praise.
Give thanks to him and bless his name.
God is good and his mercy is everlasting,
and his faithfulness is for every generation.

I will praise goodness and right;
O God, I will sing your praises with music.
I will do wisely and honestly;
when will you come to me?
I shall live in my house in sincerity of heart.
I shall desire nothing ignoble:
I have hated the action of the dishonest,
I will not stand it.
The man with a crooked heart will not be close to me
and the wicked man will not be my friend.
I will abandon the man who lies about his neighbours
     secretly.
I will not tolerate the proud-eyed man or the proud-hearted
     man.
My desire is with the honest on earth,
and for them to live with me;
the man who is upright will be my servant.
The tricky man will not live in my house,
the liar will not remain in my sight.
In the mornings I will exile all the wicked on earth
and all the unjust from the city of God.

God hear my prayer: I will cry out to you.
Do not hide your face from me on the day of my distress,
listen to me on the day I cry out and answer me,
because my days have wasted away like smoke
and my bones have burnt away like embers.
My heart is dead grass, it has withered,
I have forgotten to eat,
and my flesh has stuck to my bones
because of my groaning.
I am like the crow in the desert
and like the owl in the ruins;
I sit awake wailing alone
like a bird on the roof.
My enemies insult me the whole day,
those who are furious with me have made a conspiracy.
I have eaten ashes,
I have drunk my tears,
because of your displeasure and anger,
because you have lifted me up and thrown me down.
My days are a long shadow,
I am withering like grass.
O God, you will live for ever
and the remembrance of God in every generation.
You will rise and be merciful to Zion,
because her time of grace has come
and her appointed hour;
because your servants have loved her stones
and they have pitied her dust;
and all the nations shall fear the name of God
and every king on earth shall fear his glory.

When God built Zion
he was seen in his glory,
he heard the prayers of the poor,
he did not despise their prayers.
This shall be written for a new generation,
and a people still to be created shall praise God.
Because he has looked down from the height of his holy
    place,
God has looked out of heaven at the earth,
to hear the groaning of prisoners
and to set free the condemned to death,
to speak the name of God in Zion
and his praises in Jerusalem,
in the gathering of the peoples and kingdoms
for the service of God.
He has brought my strength to nothing on the road,
he has shortened the days of my life.
I shall say: My God, do not destroy me in half the number
    of my days.
Your years are all generations.
Long ago you made the earth
and heaven is the work of your hands;
they shall fade away and you will remain,
they shall perish like cloth,
you shall change them like a coat and they shall be changed;
you are the same,
your years never end;
and the sons of your servants shall live
and their seed shall continue in your presence.

My spirit, bless God;
everything in me, bless his name and holiness.
My spirit, bless God; remember all his graces;
who forgives all your sins and cures all your illnesses;
who rescues your life from the chasm
and crowns your head with goodness and pity;
who fills up your wishes with good things,
and your youth is as fresh as an eagle's.
God makes justice and right for all the oppressed.
He shows his road to Moses and his work to the sons of
Israel.
God is compassionate and good,
slow to anger and very merciful.
He has not handled us according to our offences
or dealt with us according to our sins.
His mercy has been powerful to those who fear him
and like the height of the heavens above the earth.
He has put our sins as far away as the east is from the west.
God has pitied those who fear him as a father pities his
children
because he knows our nature,
he is conscious that we are dust.
The life of a man is like grass,
he opens like a flower in the fields;
the wind blows and the flower is gone,
and the place where it was has forgotten it.
But the goodness of God is from everlasting to everlasting
to those who fear him;
his justice continues to the sons of their sons,
to those who keep his agreement,

who remember to do what God has commanded.
God has put his throne in the heavens,
he is universal king.
Angels of mighty power, bless God,
who carry out his words, who listen to his voice.
All his armies and the servants of his pleasure, bless God.
All his works in every part of his provinces, bless God.
My spirit, bless God.

Bless God, my spirit:
O God my God, you are very great,
you are dressed in glory and majesty,
you have covered yourself with light for your clothing,
you spread the heavens like a cloth.
The waters are the rafters of his rooms,
a storm cloud is his chariot,
he moves on the wings of the wind,
he makes the winds his messengers and blazing flames his
    servants.
He built the earth on its base and it will not be shifted for
    ever.
You have covered yourself in a cloak of deep water
and the waters shall stand up above the mountains.
They shall scatter because you speak angrily,
they shall run away quickly from the voice of your
    thunder;
and mountains shall come up and valleys shall drop down
    to the place you have made for them.
You have put limits and they will not pass
or go aside to smother the earth.
You have sent down streams into the valleys
to run between the mountains;
they water every beast of the country,
the wild ass quenches his thirst,
and the birds of the sky live beside the streams
and speak among the leaves.
You pour water from your palace onto the mountains
and the earth is filled with the produce of your work.

You grow grass for animals and green things for the service
   of man,
to get his bread from the earth,
and wine to gladden the heart of man
and oil to make his face shine;
and bread will strengthen him.
The trees of God will prosper,
the cedars of Lebanon which he planted,
and the birds nest in them
and the stork's house is in the pine-trees,
and wild goats are in the high mountains,
and the marmots have their refuge in the crags of the rocks.
You created the moon for the reckoning of time,
and the sun knows when to set.
You spread out darkness and night comes,
and every beast of the woods goes out in it:
the young lions roar for their prey,
looking to God for their food,
and when the sun rises they return together
and lie down in their dwelling.
A man shall go out to his work and his labour until the
   evening.
O God, how many your works are;
you have made them all wisely.
The earth is full of your creatures,
and what moves in the spaces of the great and wide sea is
   impossible to be numbered,
both the great and the small creatures;
the ships move on it
and you have made Leviathan to have his sport in it.
And they all look up to you
to give them food at their feeding time.
You give it and they gather it,

you open your hand and they are filled with good things.
If you hide your face they are appalled,
you take their breath and they die and go back to their dust;
you send out your breath and they are created,
you renew the face of the earth.
The glory of God shall be everlasting,
and God shall be glad because of his works.
He looks at the earth and it shivers,
he touches the tops of mountains and they smoke.
I will sing to God all my life,
I will praise my God with music while I am alive.
My thoughts of him will be delightful,
I shall be glad because of God.
Sinners shall disappear from the earth
and there shall be no more wicked.
Bless God, my spirit.
Praise God.

105

Thank God and utter his name:
declare what he has done among the peoples.
Sing to him, sing to him with the harp;
speak of all his wonderful works.
Be proud of his holy name;
those who search for God will be gladdened in their hearts.
Look for God and for his strength,
look for his face always.
Remember his wonderful works
which he has made,
and his wonders and his judgements.
Seed of his servant Abraham, chosen sons of Jacob:
He is God, he is our God,
the judge of the whole earth;
he remembers his agreement for ever,
he has spoken his command to a thousand generations:
what he agreed with Abraham, what he swore to Isaac,
    what he made law for Jacob;
a treaty with Israel for ever;
when he said, I shall give you Canaan
for the lands of your nation.
They were a handful of men,
a small number of strangers
moving from one nation to another
between kingdoms and between peoples,
but God suffered no man to oppress them,
and punished kings because of them.
You shall neither touch my anointed people, nor hurt my
    prophets.
And God commanded a famine over the earth,

and broke every loaf.
He sent a man ahead of them:
Joseph, who was sold as a slave.
They hurt his feet with fetters
and the iron went into his soul,
until the time when his words came true
and God spoke and proved him.
The king sent and set him loose,
the lord of the peoples sent and set him free.
He made him the chief man of his house
and governor of all his possessions,
to command his young princes at his pleasure
and to teach his old men wisdom.
And Israel went into Egypt,
and Jacob lived as a foreigner in the country of Ham.
And God made his people very fruitful
and stronger than their enemies.
He disturbed their hearts to hate his people
and to act cunningly against his servants.
He sent Moses his servant and Aaron whom he had chosen,
and they worked his miracles among them,
and they declared his signs among them,
and his miracles in the country of Ham.
He commanded darkness and it was dark,
and they resisted his command.
He turned their water into blood and he slaughtered their
    fish
and he increased frogs in their country
even in the rooms of their kings;
he spoke, and there were swarms of flies and mosquitoes in
    all their country;
he turned their rain to hail and blazing fire over all their
    land;

he struck their vines and fig-trees
and broke down the trees in their country;
he spoke, and there were locusts and crickets, too many to
    number,
and they ate up all the grass on their land,
and everything that grew in the ground;
and he struck the first-born of the whole country,
the first-fruit of their strength.
He brought them away with silver and with gold,
and among their tribes no man stumbled,
and Egypt was glad when they went
because they were terrified of them.
He spread out a cloud to cover them
and a fire to give them light at night.
They asked and he brought them quails,
and he filled them up with the bread of heaven,
he broke open the rock and water streamed out of it,
    running like a river in the desert,
because he remembered his holy promise to his servant
    Abraham,
and he brought away his people rejoicing,
his chosen ones shouting with happiness,
and he gave them the territories of nations,
and they inherited the labour of peoples
so that they should keep his commandments
and maintain his laws.
Praise God.

106

Praise God, thank God, because he is good
and his mercy is everlasting.
Who will describe the power of God?
Who will exhaust his praise?
I bless the just man
who does right at all times.
O God, remember me in the love of your people,
have me in your protection,
to see the happiness of your chosen,
to rejoice in the joy of your nation,
and be proud of your own people.
We have sinned like our fathers,
we have done wickedly and wrong.
Our fathers in Egypt, not understanding your wonders
nor remembering your great mercy,
rebelled at the sea, at the Sea of Reeds,
and God saved them because of his honour,
to make his strength known:
he struck the Sea of Reeds and it was dried up,
and he made them walk through the bottom of it like a desert.
He set them free from those who hated them
and rescued them from the hands of their enemies,
whom the waters drowned and not one of them was left.
And they believed in his words and sang his praises.
They went away quickly and forgot his work,
they did not wait for his wisdom.
They desired terribly in the wilderness,
they tempted God in the desert,
and he gave them what they asked for
and afflicted their spirits with a wasting fever.

They were jealous of Moses in their camp
and of Aaron the holy one of God;
and the earth opened and swallowed down Dathan
and smothered Abiram and his followers;
and a fire blazed up among them and the flames burned the
    wicked.
They made a calf in Horeb, and worshipped the metal
    image,
and they gave up their glory for the likeness of a grass-
    eating bullock;
they forgot the God of their freedom,
who did greatly in Egypt,
miracles in the country of Ham
and terrible things at the Sea of Reeds.
And he said he would annihilate them,
but Moses his chosen one faced him in the doorway,
to turn away his anger from destroying them.
And they rejected the good country,
not believing his promise;
they muttered in their tents,
not listening to the voice of God;
and he raised his hand against them to blast them in the
    desert,
to disperse their seed among the nations
and scatter them among countries.
And they gave themselves to the Baal of Peor,
and ate the meat of dead gods.
Their practices provoked God
and the plague broke out among them,
Phineas came and stood between
and the plague ceased:
and this was counted as virtue in him
for all generations and for ever.

And they provoked God at the waters of Dispute,
and harm came to Moses because of them,
because they embittered his spirit and he spoke rashly.
They did not slaughter the peoples as God commanded
them,
they mixed among the nations and learned their practices,
they served their statues and they were ensnared.
They slaughtered their sons and their daughters in sacrifice
to devils.
They poured out innocent blood:
it was the blood of their sons and their daughters;
they sacrificed them to the statues of Canaan
and the earth was polluted with the blood.
They were filthy in their action
and they were whores in their practices.
And God was very angry with his people, and loathed his
inheritance:
he put them into the hands of the nations,
those who hated them ruled them,
their enemies persecuted them and they were subject to
their hands.
Many times over he rescued them,
but they rebelled, they convinced themselves,
they were brought very low in their wickedness.
And he saw their distress and heard their crying,
and he remembered his treaty with them,
and by the greatness of his mercy he repented,
and showed them kindness in the sight of all their slave-
masters.
O God our God, save us,
and gather us together from the nations,
to thank your name which is holy,
to praise you proudly.

Bless God, the God of Israel,
from everlasting to everlasting,
and all the people shall say, Amen.
Praise God.

107

Thank God for his goodness: his mercy continues for ever.
Those that God has rescued will say so,
whom he rescued from the hands of their enemies
and gathered together out of countries,
from the east and from the west, from the north and from
    the sea.
They were wanderers in wild places in the desert,
they could not find a road to a lasting city,
they were hungry and thirsty and their spirit was fainting
and they cried out to God in distress;
and he rescued them from their troubles,
and guided them by a good road
to a lasting city.
They will thank God because of his goodness
and his wonderful work for the sons of man,
because he has satisfied desire
and filled up hunger with good things.
Who were in darkness and in the shadow of death,
in fetters of misery and of iron,
having disobeyed the commands of God
and despised the warnings of God,
and he crushed their hearts with suffering;
they stumbled and there was no one to help.
And they cried out to God in distress.
He will save them in their trouble,
he will lead them out from darkness and the shadow of
    death,
he will break their fetters to pieces,
and they will thank God because of his goodness
and his wonderful work for the sons of man.

Because he has broken down the doors of bronze
and snapped the bars of iron.
The foolish will suffer for their wrong road
because of their injustice.
They loathed every food
and they came down to the gates of death,
and they cried out to God in distress.
He will save them in their trouble,
he will send out his word and cure them
and rescue them from the pit they fell into.
They will thank God because of his goodness
and his wonderful work for the sons of man.
They will offer sacrifices of praise
and declare the action of God aloud and with shouting.
Those that go down to the sea in ships
and labour in the great waters
have seen the works of God
and his wonders in deep water.
He spoke, and a storm of wind arose
and the waves were lifted up high.
They are flung up at the sky and down to deep places,
and their souls melt with suffering.
They reel about and stagger like drunkards,
and their knowledge is eaten away to nothing.
And they cried out to God in distress,
and he will bring them out of their troubles.
He makes the storm be still,
and the waves are quiet.
And they were very glad because it was calm,
and he brought them to the harbour of their wishes.
They will thank God because of his goodness
and his wonderful work for the sons of man.

They will glorify him in the assembly of his people
and praise him in the council of old men.
He changes rivers into a wilderness,
and springs of water into barren ground,
and fruitful earth into salty land,
because of the wickedness of the people on it;
and he brings the hungry to live there
and they build a lasting city,
they sow the fields and they plant vines and the fruit increases.
And God has blessed them and greatly increased them,
and their beasts will not weaken.
They weakened and their heads drooped from oppression
and wrong and grief:
the despiser of princes made them wanderers in the desert
and there was no road;
and he lifted up the poor out of their miseries,
he fed families like flocks.
The upright shall see it and be glad
and the mouth of injustice is stopped up.
Who is wise and will keep this,
and consider the goodness of God?

O God my heart is steady,
I will sing and praise God with music, which is my glory.
Wake, lyre and harp;
I will wake at dawn and give thanks to you, O God, among
    the peoples,
I will sing with the harp among the nations.
Because your love is above the heavens and your truth is
    like the sky.
O God, be high above the heavens, and your glory over the
    whole earth.
Rescue your beloved ones,
save us with your hand and answer me.
God has spoken in his holy place:
I will take my pleasure;
I will distribute Shechem,
I will divide up the valley of Succoth,
Gilead is mine, Manasseh is mine,
Ephraim is my helmet, Judah is my sceptre,
Moab is my washpot, I throw down my shoe on Edom,
I will shout over the Philistines.
Who will bring me into the fortified city?
Who has led me into Edom?
Was it not you, God, who rejected us?
and who will not go out with our armies, O God?
Help us in trouble,
human help is an empty thing.
Through God we shall do mightily,
and he will tread down our enemies.

God of my praise, do not be silent,
because the wicked and the deceitful have opened their
    mouths against me,
they have spoken with lying tongues
and assaulted me with words of hatred,
they have fought me without cause.
I was their friend, they were my accusers,
and I cry to God:
I gave them good, they gave me harm,
I loved them and they hated me.
Give a wicked man charge of him,
put an enemy at his right hand,
in court he will be found guilty
and his crying out will prove the crime.
His time will be short, and another man will have his place,
his sons will be orphaned and his wife widowed,
his sons will be wanderers and beggars,
and rag-pickers living in the ruins of houses.
The money-lender will trap all he owns,
and strangers will take loot from his labour.
Let no man continue to be good to him,
nor decent to his children;
let his family be extinguished
and their name blotted out in one generation.
Let God remember the wickedness of his fathers,
and the sins of his mother not be wiped away,
let them be in God's sight always
and let God destroy their memory out of the earth.
He never thought of mercy,
he hunted down the destitute and poor

and the broken-hearted to their death.
He loved cursing, and it came on him,
he hated blessing, and it stayed away from him.
And he was dressed in curses like clothing,
they entered him like water,
they soaked into his bones like oil.
Let it be his dress to cover him and his belt to go round him
     always.
This is the wages of God to my enemies
who talk wickedly against my life.
O God, deal with me according to your name,
save me because of your goodness and mercy,
because I am destitute and poor and my heart is hurt,
I am far gone, I am a long shadow.
I am shaking like a cricket,
my knees have failed because I have not eaten,
and the fat has withered in my flesh.
I have been a word for them to curse with,
they look at me and wag their heads.
O God my God, help me,
save me in your mercy;
they will know it is your hand;
O God, you have done it.
They curse and you bless;
they will stand up and be ashamed
and your servant will be glad.
My enemies will be dressed in dishonour,
they will cover themselves in shame like a cloak;
I will thank God in my words very greatly,
I will praise him among many people,
because he stands at the right hand of the destitute
to save his life from the judges.

God said to my lord:
Sit at my right hand,
and I will make your enemies a stool for your feet.
God shall send out from Zion the sceptre of your strength;
rule among your enemies.
Your people desire the day of your power in the majesty
    of holiness,
and your young men are dew from the womb of dawn.
God has sworn and will not repent:
You are a priest for ever in the order of Melchizedek.
God will shatter kings at your right hand on the day of his
    anger.
He will judge the nations;
he will heap up dead;
he will scatter the great far across country.
He will drink from the stream on his road,
and then he will lift up his head.

III

Praise God.
I will thank God with my whole heart
in the senate of the just and the assembly.
The works of God are very great
and studied by all who love them.
His work is glory and majesty
and his justice is for ever.
The wonder of his works is a witness:
God is good and very merciful.
He provides for those that fear him,
he will remember his agreement for ever.
He has shown his powerful working to his people
and given them the nations for an inheritance.
Truth and right are the work of his hands
and all his commands are steady:
they are for ever, he created them in truth and right.
He rescued his people,
he commanded his law for ever,
his name is holy and fearful.
The fear of God is the beginning of wisdom
and understanding belongs to those who keep his law.
His praise continues for ever.

Praise God.
I bless the man who fears God,
who has pleasure in his law:
his seed will be mighty on the earth,
the upright generation will be blessed.
His house will have riches and precious things,
and his justice will continue for ever.
Light for the just has risen in the darkness,
which is good and merciful and upright.
The good man is decent and generous,
he furthers his affairs rightly.
He will never be shifted,
the just man will be remembered for ever.
He will not fear wicked talk,
his heart is strong and he trusts God:
his heart is fixed, he is not afraid,
he will see the shame of his persecutors.
He scattered his goods and gave to the destitute,
his uprightness continues for ever,
his head shall be gloriously lifted up.
The wicked man shall see it and be sorry,
he shall grind his teeth and wither,
the wicked man's wishes will come to nothing.

Praise God,
servants of God praise God,
praise the name of God.
Bless the name of God now and for ever.
From the rising of the sun to the setting of the sun
praise the name of God.
God is very high above all the nations
and his glory is above the heavens.
Who is like God, our God?
Who lives in the height,
who bows down low to see the heavens and the earth,
who picks up the destitute from the dust,
and lifts the poor from dunghills,
and sits them down among princes,
among the princes of his nation.
He brings in the barren woman to live in her own house,
to be happy and a mother of sons.
Praise God.

When Israel went out from Egypt,
and the house of Jacob from a people of stammerers,
Judah was his holy place, Israel was his kingdom.
The sea saw him and fled
and Jordan ran backwards,
the mountains skipped like rams
and the little hills like lambs.
Why was it, O sea, that you fled?
O Jordan, that you ran backwards?
O mountains, that you skipped like rams?
O little hills, like lambs?
O world, be troubled in the sight of God,
in the sight of the God of Jacob:
who changes the rock into pools of water
and granite into springs of water.

Give glory to your **name**, O God,
but not to us, not to us,
by your mercy and by your faithfulness.
Why do the nations say, Where is their God?
Our God is in the heavens,
he does what delights him.
Their statues are of silver and gold,
the work of the hands of men,
they have mouths and cannot speak,
they have eyes and cannot see,
they have ears and cannot hear,
they have noses and cannot smell,
they have hands and cannot feel,
they have feet and cannot walk;
their throats are silent.
Let the makers of them be like them,
and the same with everyone who trusts them.
O Israel, trust God:
he is their help and their shield.
House of Aaron, trust God:
he is their help and their shield.
All who fear him, trust God:
he is their help and their shield.
God has remembered us, he shall bless us;
he shall bless the house of Israel;
he shall bless the house of Aaron;
he shall bless all who fear him, great and small.
God will increase you and increase your sons,
God who made the heavens and the earth has blessed you.

All the heavens belong to God
and he gave the earth to the sons of man.
The dead will not praise God,
they go down into the country of silence.
We will bless God now and for ever.
Praise God.

I have loved God
because he hears my voice and my crying,
because he listens to me when I cry to him.
The ropes of death were round me
and the grip of Hell had me,
I suffered and grieved, and I called God by his name,
O God, I beg you to rescue my life.
God is kindly and upright; our God is merciful;
God guards the simple;
I have been brought down and he will save me.
Go back to rest, my soul,
because God has been good to you.
He has saved my soul from death and my eyes from tears
　　and my feet from failing;
I will walk in the sight of God in the fields of the living.
I have trusted him and I say:
I was brought down very low;
and I said in my confusion:
All men are betrayers.
What shall I give back to God
for all his mercies to me?
I will lift up the cup of freedom,
and call to God by his name.
I will pay my promises to God
in the sight of all his nation.
The death of his holy ones is precious in the sight of God.
O God, I am your servant,
I am your slave and I was born your slave;
you have taken off the fetters of death.

I will bring you sacrifices of praise
and call to God by his name.
I will pay my promises to God
in the sight of all his nation,
in the courtyards of the house of God,
in the middle of you, O Jerusalem.
Praise God.

117

Praise God, all nations;
praise him, all people;
because his mercy has been strong over us,
and God is faithful for ever.
Praise God.

Thank God because he is good,
and his mercy continues for ever.
Let Israel say: His mercy continues for ever.
Let the house of Aaron say: His mercy continues for ever.
Let all who fear him say: His mercy continues for ever.
I cried out to God in a narrow place
and he answered me in freedom.
God is for me, I will not be afraid:
what will man do to me?
God is for me, God is on my side,
I will confront my enemies.
It is better to trust God
than be confident in men.
It is better to trust God
than be confident in princes.
All nations came around me;
in the name of God I will destroy them.
They came around me and around me,
and in the name of God I will destroy them.
They came round me like bees,
I put them out like a fire of thorns;
in the name of God I will destroy them.
They pushed to push me over,
and God helped me.
God is my strength and my music,
he has been my freedom.
The voices of shouting and freedom in the tents of the just:
the right hand of God works mightily,
the right hand of God is lifted up,
the right hand of God works mightily.

I shall not die but live
and speak of the work of God.
God has punished me and not let me die.
Open to me, gates of justice:
I will go in by them and praise God.
This is the gate of God, the just shall go in by it.
I will offer my thanks because you have heard me,
and you have been my freedom.
The stone that the builders despised is the best stone in the
    wall.
This is the work of God,
and it was marvellous to us.
This is the day that God has made;
we will rejoice on this day and be very glad.
O God, I beg you set us free;
O God, I beg you make us rich.
I bless whoever comes in the name of God:
we have blessed you from the house of God.
God is God who shone his light on us.
Rope the sacrifice to the altar-horns.
You are my God and I will thank you;
O my God, I will praise you greatly.
Thank God because he is good,
because his mercy continues for ever.

Happy is the honest man
who walks by the law of God.
Happy are those who keep his code
and look for him with all their hearts;
who have done no wickedness
and have walked in his road.
You have commanded your laws to be well kept,
and I shall not be ashamed of the study of all your instructions.
I will thank you in honesty of heart
and by learning the judgements of your justice.
I will keep your decrees;
do not utterly abandon me.

How shall a young man purify his path
to keep to your command?
I have looked for you with all my heart;
do not let me wander from your instructions.
I have hidden your sayings in my heart,
therefore I will not sin against you.
I bless you, O God; teach me your decrees.
My lips have repeated all the judgements you have spoken,
I have rejoiced in the ways of your code,
like absolute wealth.
I will consider your laws, and study your paths,
I will delight in your doctrine,
I will remember your command.

Do good to your servant; I shall live and keep your
    commands.
Open my eyes and I shall see the wonders of your law.

I am a stranger on earth; do not hide your instructions from
me.
My spirit has been crushed with desire of your judgements
at all times.
You have punished the proud; unhappy are those who
stray from your instructions.
Take away contempt and derision from me; I have kept
your code.
Princes have taken their seats and spoken against me; your
servant will consider your decrees.
Your code is my pleasure and my parliament.

My soul is stuck in the dust; make me live by your com-
mands.
I have told you my paths and you have answered me;
teach me your decrees,
and to contemplate the path of your laws
and meditate the wonders of your work.
My spirit has dropped down with heaviness;
lift me by your commands.
Put the path of deceit far away from me,
and grant me your law.
I have chosen the faithful path,
I have abided by your judgements.
I have stuck to your code;
O God, do not dishonour me.
I will run on the path of your instructions
because you will make my heart free.

O God, teach me the path of your decrees
and I will keep to it to the end.
Make my spirit see and I will keep your law
and observe it with all my heart.

Guide me on the path of your statutes
because it has been my pleasure.
Draw my heart to your code and not to profit.
Turn my eyes from vanities,
make me live by your commands.
Put your sayings in the sight of your servant
because he fears you.
Take away my punishment because I am afraid,
and because your judgements are merciful.
I have desired your laws;
make me live by your justice.

O God, your mercy and salvation will come to me
according to your sayings.
I will answer words of insult
because I have trusted the word of your commands.
Do not take away the words of truth from my mouth;
I have longed for your judgements.
I will keep your law always:
for ever and ever.
And I shall walk in freedom, because I have looked for your
    laws.
I have spoken by your code in the sight of kings,
and I shall not be ashamed.
I shall take pleasure in your instructions which I have loved.
I will lift up my hands to your laws, which I have loved.
I will meditate your decrees.

Remember your command to your servant,
in which you have made me hope.
This is my comfort in miseries; your sayings have saved my
    life.

The proud have utterly despised me
and I have not dropped away from your law.
O God, I have remembered your ancient judgements
and have been comforted.
I was overwhelmed with horror
because the wicked have deserted your law.
Your decrees were my music in my house.
O God, I have remembered your name in the night,
and I will keep your law.
This has been mine: I have guarded your laws.

My possession is God;
I have said I will keep to the word of his commands.
I begged him with all my heart: Be merciful to me accord-
    ing to your sayings.
I have considered my paths, and turned to your code,
I ran quickly to keep your instructions.
The ropes of the wicked were round me, but I have
    remembered your law;
and at midnight I will wake and thank you
for the judgements of your justice.
I am the friend of all who fear you
and everyone who keeps your laws.
O God, the earth has been filled with your mercy;
teach me your decrees.

O God, you have been good to your servant
according to the prophecies of your commands.
Teach me goodness of judgement and knowledge
because I have believed in your instructions.
I was ignorant until I was brought down,
and now I have observed your sayings.
But you are good and do good; teach me your decrees.

The proud have built up lies against me,
but I will keep your laws with all my heart.
Their hearts are as fat as meat;
I have been delighted with your law.
It was good for me to be brought down
because I will learn your decrees;
the law in your mouth is good for me,
and better than great quantities of gold and of silver.

Your hands made me and strengthened me;
give me understanding and I will learn your instructions.
Those who fear you will see me and be glad
because my hope has been in your commands.
O God, I know that your judgements are justice;
you humbled me according to your promise.
Give me your mercy to comfort me,
according to your sayings to your servant.
Your great kindness will come to me and I will live,
because your law is my delight.
The proud will be ashamed, because they twisted me with
    deceits,
but I will meditate your laws.
Those who fear you and know your code will turn to me;
my heart will be upright in your decrees
and therefore I will not be dishonoured.

My spirit has withered for your freedom;
I have hoped for your command.
My eyes have withered for your sayings.
I have said, When will you comfort me?
I have wept like a wine-skin in the smoke,
but I remembered your decrees.
What is the lifetime of your servant?

When will you judge my persecutors?
The proud have dug ditches for me to fall in,
against your law.
All your instructions are faithfulness; help me:
they have pursued me with treachery,
they came near to destroying me from the earth.
I have not abandoned your laws;
let me live by your mercy,
and I will keep the code you have given.

O God, your command stands in the heavens for ever,
you are faithful in every generation;
you have set up the earth and it stands,
it stands by your judgement every day;
everything is your servant.
If your law had not been my delight
I should have perished in my misery.
I will never forget your laws
because you gave me life in them.
I belong to you; set me free
because I have looked for your laws.
The wicked have waited for me to destroy me;
I will keep my mind on your code.
I have seen the limit of every perfection,
but your instructions are freedom.

I have loved your law,
I have meditated it all day long.
By your instructions you make me wiser than my enemies
because they are mine for ever.
I have understood more than all my teachers
because I have meditated your code.

I can think more than the old
because I have guarded your laws.
I have kept back from all the paths of evil
because I keep to your commands.
I have not gone away from your judgements
because you have taught me.
Your sayings have been sweet in my mouth
and better than honey in my mouth.
I think by your laws,
and therefore I have hated all the paths of deceit.

Your command is a lamp for my steps and a light for my
    path.
I have sworn and established this:
to keep to the judgements of your justice.
I have been very much humbled;
O God, guard my life according to your commands.
O God, be pleased with the free offerings of my words
and teach me your judgements.
My life is always in my hands
and I have remembered your law.
The wicked put down a trap for me
and I have not gone away from your laws.
Your code is my possession for ever
and it cheers my heart.
I have set my heart to carry out your decrees for ever
until the end.

I have hated doubts and loved your law.
You are my hiding-place, you are my shield;
I have hoped for your commands.
Go away from me, you wrongdoers;
I will keep the instructions of my God.

Support me and I shall be free,
and I will study your decrees continually.
You have crushed all those who went away from your
  decrees,
because of the treachery of their deceits.
You have raked out all the wicked on earth like slag,
therefore I have loved your code.
My flesh has bristled for fear of you
and I have been afraid of your judgements.

I have acted in judgement and justice;
you will not leave me to my oppressors.
Witness for the defence of your servant;
do not let proud men oppress me.
My eyes have withered away for your protection
and the sayings of your justice;
deal with your servant according to your mercy,
teach me your decrees.
I am your servant; teach me to consider
and to understand your code.
It is time for God to work:
they have cancelled his law.
I have loved your instructions better than gold and refined
  gold.
I have believed that the decrees of God are right.
I have hated every deceitful path.

Your code is wonderful, therefore my spirit guards it.
The study of your commands is enlightenment,
it is the understanding of the simple.
I have opened my mouth and panted with longing for your
  instructions.
Turn to me and show me kindness, as you do to lovers of
  your name.

Strengthen my steps with your sayings,
let no injustice get command of me.
Rescue me from human oppression
and I will keep your laws.
Make your face shine on your servant
and teach me your decrees.
Waterstreams have run down from my eyes
because they have not kept your law.

O God, you are just and your judgements are upright.
You have commanded the justice of your code
and its great faithfulness.
My passion has destroyed me:
I was distressed by those who have forgotten your com-
    mands.
Your sayings are very pure,
and your servant has loved them.
I am small and abject; I have not forgotten your laws.
Your justice is everlasting justice
and your law is the faithfulness of God.
I have been in distress and suffering;
your instructions are my delight.
Your code is everlasting justice;
give me understanding and I shall live.

I have cried out with all my heart; O God answer me,
I will guard your decrees.
I have cried out to you;
rescue me and I will keep your code.
I have cried out before dawn,
I have hoped for your command,
before the night was over my eyes have studied your
    sayings.

Hear my voice according to your mercy;
O God, give me life according to your judgement.
Malicious men have come near me; they are distant from
    your law.
O God, you are near me and all your instructions are faithful.
Long ago I knew from your code
that you have established it for ever.

See my misery and rescue me
because I have not forgotten your law.
Speak for me and save me,
give me life by your sayings.
Freedom is far from the wicked
because they have not looked for your decrees.
O God, your mercies are very many;
give me life according to your judgements.
There are many who persecute me and torture me;
I have not dropped away from your code.
I have seen sinners and I suffered:
they have not kept to your sayings.
Look, I have loved your laws;
O God, give me life according to your mercy.
The sum of your commands is to be honest,
and every judgement of your justice is everlasting.

Princes have hunted me for no reason
and in my heart I have feared your commands,
I have rejoiced over your commands
like a man who finds a quantity of loot.
I have hated and abominated falseness;
I have loved your law.
I have praised you seven times a day
because of the judgements of your justice.

Those who love your law have very great peace,
and there is nothing to trip them up.
O God, I have waited for your freedom
and I have carried out your instructions.
My soul has kept your code,
I have loved it very much.
I have kept your laws and your code
because all my paths are in your sight.

O God, I will cry out and reach you;
give me understanding according to your command.
I will pray and reach you;
give me freedom according to your sayings.
My lips utter your praise
because you teach me your decrees.
My tongue replies to your sayings
because all your instructions are justice.
Your hand will help me
because I have chosen your laws.
O God, I have longed for your freedom
and your law is my delight.
My soul will live and praise you,
and your judgements will come to my help.
I have wandered like a dying sheep;
look for your servant,
because I have not forgotten your instructions.

I cried out to God in my trouble,
and he heard me.
O God, rescue me from lying lips and tricky tongues.
What should you get, what should be done to you, tricky
tongues?
Sharp arrows shot with strength, and the hot cinders of a
gorse-bush.
I wish I had never stopped in Meshech
or lived among the camps of Kedar:
my spirit has been too long among peace-hating people.
I am peaceful, but when I speak they prepare for war.

I will lift my eyes to the mountains;
how will I be helped?
My help comes from God, the maker of the heavens and the
    earth.
He shall not let your foot stumble,
he who guards you shall not sleep.
The guardian of Israel shall not sleep or be drowsy.
God guards you, and the shadow of God is on your right
    hand.
The sun shall not strike you by day
nor the moon in the night.
God will guard you from all evil,
he will guard your soul.
God will guard you in your going out
and in your coming in,
now and for everlasting.

I was glad because they said to me,
We shall go to the house of God.
We have set our feet in your gates, Jerusalem:
Jerusalem which is built as a city
united together in itself,
where the tribes come up, the tribes of God,
the witness of God to Israel to thank the name of God.
Because seats of judgement are in it,
the seats of the house of David.
Pray for the peace of Jerusalem;
those that love you shall prosper,
there shall be peace within your walls and prosperity in your
    houses.
Because of my brothers and my friends
I wish you peace.
Because of the house of God who is our God
I will pray for the good of Jerusalem.

I have lifted up my eyes to you,
God who lives in the heavens.
Like a servant watching the hand of his master,
like a girl watching the hand of her mistress,
we look to God who is our God,
and the moment of his mercy.
Be merciful to us, O God, be merciful,
because we have been too much despised,
our spirits have had too much of the mocking of the idle
and the derision of the proud.

If God had not been for us,
let Israel say,
If God had not been for us,
when man stood against us,
they would have swallowed us up living,
in the rage of their anger against us;
and the water would have covered us,
and the floods would have streamed above our souls.
The waters of their pride would have streamed above our
souls.
Bless God: he did not make us meat for their teeth.
Our souls were set free like birds out of the snares of the
bird-catcher.
Our help is the name of God
who made the heavens and the earth.

Those who trust God are like Mount Zion:
it will not be broken, it will stand for ever.
The mountains stand around Jerusalem,
and God stands around his nation
now and for ever.
The sceptre of wickedness shall not touch the inheritance of
    the just:
the hands of the just shall not touch injustice.
O God, do good to the good and the honest.
God will make those who walk in crooked roads go among
    the wicked.
Peace to Israel.

When God brought back Zion
it was like dreaming:
our mouths were full of laughing and singing,
they said among the nations:
God has done a great work with these people.
God had done a great work with us,
we have been very glad.
O God, bring us back,
like the rivers in the Negev.
Those who sow in tears shall reap in joy,
everyone who carries his basket of seed in tears
shall come back with a harvest shouting for joy.

If God will not build the house
the builders have laboured for nothing.
If God will not guard the city
the guards have kept watch for nothing.
Rising early and sitting late
and eating the bread of miseries is for nothing:
God will give his beloved sleep.
Look: your inheritance from God is sons,
your wages are the fruit of the womb.
The sons of youth are like arrows in the hand of a strong
    man.
Happy is the man who fills his quiver with them:
he will not be dishonoured
when he talks to his enemies in the gateway.

I bless every man who fears God
and walks in his paths.
You shall eat the labour of your hands,
you shall have blessings and good things;
your wife will be like a fruiting vine in the rooms of your
    house
and your sons like young olive trees around your table.
A man who fears God shall have these blessings.
God shall bless you from Zion,
you shall see the goodness of Jerusalem
through all the days of your life,
and see the sons of your sons.
Peace to Israel.

They have terribly tormented me from my youth,
let Israel say,
They have terribly tormented me from my youth,
but I never surrendered.
The ploughmen have ploughed up my back,
the furrows were very long.
God is just, he has broken the ropes of the wicked,
they shall all be ashamed and driven back
who have hated Zion;
they shall be like grass on the roof
that has withered before it grows,
and no mower takes it in his hand,
and no binder bundles it in his arms,
and no one says, passing by:
God bless you,
we bless you with the name of God.

O God, I have cried to you out of the depths;
O God, hear my voice,
listen to my voice in my prayers.
O God, if you remember sins,
God, who can stand it?
Forgiveness is with you,
therefore you shall be feared.
I have waited for God;
my spirit has waited, I have hoped for his word;
my spirit has waited for God
more than the watchers for dawn have waited for the
    dawn.
Let Israel hope in God,
because mercy is with God
and continued rescue,
and he shall rescue Israel from all his sins.

O God, my heart has not been proud or my eyes lifted up,
I have not moved among great matters or wonders which
    are above me;
I have made my spirit still and silent
like a sucking child on its mother's breast,
my spirit is a sucking child.
God is the hope of Israel
now and for ever.

O God, remember David
and all his sufferings.
He swore to God,
he promised to the strong one of Jacob:
I shall not go under cover of my house,
I shall not go to my bed,
I shall not let my eyes sleep or my eyelids be drowsy
before I get a sanctuary for God
and a place for the strong one of Jacob.
We heard of his throne in Ephrathah
and we found it in the fields of the forest.
Let us go to where he is
and worship at the stool under his feet.
O God, enter your rest
with the throne of your power.
Your priests will be dressed in justice
and your holy ones will shout and rejoice.
For the sake of David your servant
do not turn away the face of your anointed.
God swore an oath to David,
and he will not go back on it:
I will make the fruit of your body kings,
if your sons will keep my agreement
and my laws which I will teach them,
and I will make their sons in succession kings for ever.
God has chosen Zion,
he has desired it for his own place:
This is my resting-place for ever,
I shall rest here because I love this place.
I will increase the meat with blessings,

I will fill the poor with food.
I will dress the priests in freedom,
and the holy will shout and rejoice.
I will grow a horn for David.
I have lighted a lamp for my anointed.
I will dress his enemies in dishonour,
and his crown will flower on his head.

How good and delightful it is
when brothers live together,
like the good oil on the head of Aaron,
which ran down in his beard
and ran down on the edges of his vestments,
like the dew of Hermon running down on the mountains of
    Zion,
because God has commanded his blessing on them,
everlasting life.

Bless God, all the servants of God
who stand at night in the house of God.
Lift up your hands in the holy place
and bless God.
God, who made the heavens and the earth,
shall bless you from Mount Zion.

Praise God; praise the name of God;
praise him, servants of God
who stand in the house of God,
in the courts of his house.
Praise God because he is good;
praise his name with pleasant music
because God has chosen Jacob,
Israel is his treasure.
I know that God is great:
our God is greater than all gods.
God has done what delighted him
in the heavens and on earth
and on the surface of the sea and in deep water:
he brought clouds from the end of the earth,
he created lightnings for rain,
he brought out wind from his storehouses;
he struck the firstborn of Egypt,
both the men and the cattle,
he did signs and miracles among you, O Egypt,
to Pharaoh and to all his servants;
he struck many nations,
he killed mighty kings:
King Sihon of the Amorites and King Og of Bashan,
and all the kingdoms of Canaan;
and he gave their land for inheritance
to Israel his nation.
O God, your name is everlasting,
O God, you are remembered
in every generation.

God will judge his nation
and he will pity his servants.
The statues of the nations are of silver and gold,
the work of the hands of men;
they have mouths and cannot speak,
they have eyes and cannot see,
they have ears and cannot hear,
they have no breath in their mouths.
Let the makers of them be like them,
and the same with everyone who trusts them.
House of Israel, bless God;
house of Aaron, bless God;
house of Levi, bless God;
bless God in Zion who lives in Jerusalem.
Praise God.

Give thanks to God because he is good,
his mercy is everlasting;
give thanks to the God of gods,
his mercy is everlasting;
give thanks to the lord of lords,
his mercy is everlasting;
who alone does great wonders,
his mercy is everlasting;
who made the heavens in wisdom,
his mercy is everlasting;
who spread the earth on the waters,
his mercy is everlasting;
who created the great lights,
his mercy is everlasting;
the sun to be king in the day,
his mercy is everlasting;
the moon and the stars to be kings in the night,
his mercy is everlasting;
who struck the first-born of Egypt,
his mercy is everlasting;
who brought away Israel from among them,
his mercy is everlasting;
with a strong hand, with a raised arm,
his mercy is everlasting;
who split apart the sea of reeds,
his mercy is everlasting;
and guided Israel through the middle,
his mercy is everlasting;
and threw Pharaoh and his army into the sea,
his mercy is everlasting;

and guided his nation in the desert,
his mercy is everlasting;
who struck great kings,
his mercy is everlasting;
and killed glorious kings,
his mercy is everlasting;
Sihon the king of the Amorites,
his mercy is everlasting;
and Og the king of Bashan,
his mercy is everlasting;
and he gave their land for a possession,
his mercy is everlasting;
the possession of Israel his servant,
his mercy is everlasting;
who remembered us in our nothing,
his mercy is everlasting;
and tore us away from persecutors,
his mercy is everlasting;
and gives bread to every living creature,
his mercy is everlasting;
give thanks to the God of the heavens,
his mercy is everlasting.

By the streams of Babylon we sat down and wept
when we remembered Zion.
We hung up our harps on the willow trees
when the masters called for songs
and the torturers for cheerfulness:
Sing us a song from Zion.
How shall we sing the songs of God in a foreign country?
If I forget you, Jerusalem,
let my right hand forget to grip,
let my tongue stick to the roof of my mouth,
unless I remember you
and put Jerusalem above the top of my happiness.
O God, remember the last moment of Jerusalem
against the sons of Edom:
when they said, Strip it down,
strip it down to the foundations.
Daughter of Babylon, slaughterer,
I bless the man who will pay your wages
as you payed them to us.
I bless the man who will take your children
and smash them on rocks.

138

I will thank you with my whole heart,
I will praise God with music,
I will bow down at your holy temple
and thank the name of God,
because of your mercy and your faithfulness,
because you have made your promise
greater than all your names.
I cried out in the day and you answered me,
you made me very strong.
O God, all the kings of the earth shall thank you,
because they have heard your sayings.
And they shall sing on the roads of God
because of the greatness of his glory.
God is very high but he sees the poor
and knows the proud from a great distance.
If I walk in the middle of miseries
you guard my life,
you stretch out your hand against the fury of my enemies,
and your right hand will rescue me.
God will finish my business.
O God, your mercy is everlasting;
do not abandon the work of your hands.

O God, you have examined me and you know:
you know me in my sitting down and in my standing up;
you have understood my thoughts from far away;
you watch my road and my rest;
you are familiar with all my paths.
Before any word is on my tongue,
O God, you know it.
You surround me, you are in front and behind,
and your hand touches me.
This understanding is marvellous and too much for me,
it is high and I cannot grasp it.
Where shall I go from your spirit?
And where shall I hide from your face?
If I go up into the heavens you are there,
and if I lie down among the dead you are there,
if I take the wings of dawn and live in the furthest region of
    the sea,
even there your hand will guide me and your right hand
    will hold me.
And I said, Surely the darkness will cover me and the night
    will be my light.
But darkness is not dark to you,
and the night shines like the day
and the dark is light.
Because you produced my body
and covered me in the womb of my mother,
and I will thank you
because I was wonderfully and terribly created,
and my spirit knows very well
that your works are wonderful.

My bones were not hidden from you
when I was made in a secret place
and dappled with colours in the lowest parts of the earth.
Your eyes saw my unshaped body,
and everything was written in your book
with the day of its creation
before there was anything.
O God, your thoughts have been precious to me,
and their quantity is mighty.
If I number them they are more than the sand,
and I wake and I am still with you.
O God, you will certainly kill the unjust man:
go away from me, men with bloody hands.
They speak of you trickily,
they take it up for hollow reasons, your enemies.
O God, shall I not hate those that hate you?
And be angry with your enemies?
I have hated them with complete hate,
they have been my enemies.
O God, examine me and know my heart,
try me and know my thoughts,
and see if any bad road is in me,
and guide me by an everlasting road.

O God, rescue me from wicked men,
protect me from violent men:
they dream up evil in their hearts,
they pick quarrels all day long,
they sharpen their tongues like snakes
and they have snake-poison on their lips.
God, keep me from the hands of the unjust man
and save me from the violent who have planned to trip me
    up.
The proud have made a hidden trap with ropes,
they have spread out a net by the roadside,
they have put down snares for me.
I said to God, You are my God,
O God, hear my prayer:
O God, my strong freedom,
cover my head on the day of battle.
O God, let the unjust man not have his wishes,
make his trick fail,
let them not win.
Let their chief men suffer by the offence of their own
    mouths.
Let blazing coal drop on them,
let them fall into pits and not rise,
let the clever tongue not live on the earth,
let evil dog the violent man and drag him down.
I know that God will take up the poor man's business
and the rights of the destitute.
The just will thank you by your name,
and the innocent will live in your sight.

God, I cry out to you; come quickly
and listen to my voice.
My prayers shall continue like incense in your sight,
and the lifting up of my hands like the evening sacrifice.
O God, put a guard on my mouth,
keep the door of my lips.
Do not turn my heart to evil things,
and wicked practices and unjust men;
let me not eat their delicious food.
If the just man strikes me it is a mercy,
if he punishes me it is oil on my head:
it will never break my head
because I pray continually in sufferings.
If their judges were flung off a cliff
they would hear my words and find them pleasant.
It has been like slashing and chopping in the fields:
our bones have been flung down into the opening of Hell.
My eyes are on you, O God,
I have trusted you;
do not strip my soul bare.
Keep me out of the trap which they put down for me,
and out of the snares of the unjust.
The wicked shall all fall into their own nets,
and I shall go forward.

I will cry out to God, I will pray to God;
I will tell him my thoughts, I will show him my miseries.
My spirit is agonized;
you know my road.
They have put a trap in the road I shall walk;
look on the right hand and see, there is no one who knows.
I have nowhere to run to, there is no one who cares for me.
O God, I have cried to you;
I have said, You are my refuge
and my possessions in the land of the living.
Listen to my crying
because I have been brought very low.
Rescue me from the hunt
because they are stronger than I am.
Bring my spirit out of prison
to thank you by your name.
The just will be all around me
because you will pay me my wages.

143

God, hear my prayer, listen to my prayer,
answer me with justice according to your faithfulness.
Do not bring your servant to judgement
because no living creature is just in your sight.
Enemies have hunted down my soul,
they have crushed my life on the ground
and sent me to live in dark places among the ancient dead.
My spirit is agonized and my heart has wasted.
I have remembered ancient times,
I have considered all your actions,
I will meditate the work of your hands.
I have stretched out my hands to you,
my spirit is a barren country looking up to you.
O God, come quickly and answer;
my spirit has withered away.
Do not hide your face from me,
or I shall be like those that go down into the grave.
Let me hear of your mercy in the morning
because I have trusted you;
let me know the road to walk by
because I have raised up my spirit to you.
Rescue me from my enemies;
O God, you have been my shelter.
Instruct me to do your pleasure, because you are my God,
and your good spirit shall guide me through a flat country.
O God, in your honour guard my life,
in your justice bring my spirit out of misery,
in your mercy strike my enemies,
and destroy the tormentors of my spirit,
because I am your servant.

Bless God; he is my mountain,
he teaches my hands war
and my fingers how to fight.
He is my help and my defences,
and my hill-fort and my rescuer.
He is my shield and I trust him,
he keeps down peoples under me.
O God, what is man that you should know him?
Or the son of man that you should think of him?
Man is a kind of nothing,
his days are like a shadow that goes past.
O God, bend the heavens and come down;
touch the tops of the mountains and they will smoke;
let lightnings lighten and scatter,
shoot arrows and let them storm,
put down your hand from the height,
rescue me and set me free
from the mass of waters
and the hands of strangers:
their mouths talk nonsense
and their right hands are treacherous.
O God, I will sing you a new song
with music of ten strings,
I will sing your praises with the harp.
God gives freedom to kings
and rescues his servant David
from the sword of evil.
Rescue me and set me free from the hands of strangers:
their mouths talk nonsense
and their right hands are treacherous.

May our sons be like trees growing tall in their youth,
may our daughters be like special stones cut for palaces,
and our sheds be full of every kind of stores,
and our sheep have lambs in thousands and tens of thou-
    sands in the fields,
and our cattle be pregnant without hurt or miscarriage,
and no one be lamenting in our streets.
Happy is the nation like this,
happy is the nation which has God for its god.

I will praise you, my God and king,
I will bless your name for ever and ever.
God is great and his praise is great,
his greatness cannot be found out.
Every generation shall praise your works
and speak of your mightiness;
I will meditate your majesty and glory and honour
and the wonders of your works.
They shall say that the strength of your work is terrible;
I will declare your greatness.
They shall remember your great goodness
and shout with joy because of your justice.
God is good and merciful,
slow to anger and great in mercy.
God is good to all creation
and his love reaches to all his work.
O God, all your works shall thank you
and your holy ones shall bless you.
They shall speak of your glorious kingdom
and your mightiness:
to make the power of God known among men,
and his glory and majesty and kingdom.
Your kingdom is a kingdom of everlasting ages
and your reign is through every generation.
God holds up the fallen
and he lifts up all those who are down.
The eyes of all creatures look up to you,
you have given them food at their feeding-time.
You open your hand and fill everything living with
    delight.

God is just on all his roads
and holy in all his work.
God is close to anyone who cries out to him,
who cries out to him in honesty.
He does the desires of those who fear him,
he hears them crying and he rescues them.
God guards all those who love him,
and destroys the wicked.
I will open my mouth to praise God,
and every living creature shall bless the name of his holiness
for ever and for ever.

Praise God;
O my soul, praise God;
I will praise God in my life,
I will sing to my God with the harp while I live.
Have no confidence in princes or in any son of man,
in whom there is no salvation.
His breath will go out of him, he will go back to earth;
on that day all his thoughts will perish.
I bless the man whose help is the God of Jacob,
whose trust is in God who is his God,
who made the heavens and the earth
and the sea and everything in them,
who keeps his promise for ever,
who judges for the oppressed,
who gives bread to the hungry.
God unties prisoners,
God opens the eyes of the blind,
God lifts up everyone bowed down,
God loves the just,
God guards the stranger,
he helps widows and the fatherless,
he twists the road under the wicked.
God shall reign for ever,
O Zion, your God in every generation.
Praise God.

Praise God because he is good.
Praise our God with music because he is pleased with it:
praise is pleasant.
God is building Jerusalem:
he will gather the scattered of Israel,
he cures the broken-hearted and dresses their wounds,
he counts the numbers of the stars
and calls them all by name.
God is great and very powerful,
his knowledge cannot be counted.
God raises up the miserable, and crushes the wicked on the
    earth.
Reply to God with thanks,
praise our God with music and with the harp.
He covers over heaven with clouds
and makes rain for the earth,
he makes the grass spring up on the mountains
and gives food to the animals
and the tribes of the crows when they cry out.
His pleasure is not in the power of horses,
nor is it in the legs of men,
the delight of God is everyone who fears him
and everyone whose hope is his mercy.
Praise God, Jerusalem,
praise your God, Zion:
because he has made the bars of your gates powerful
and blessed your sons in the city,
he has made your frontiers peace
and feeds you full with the richness of wheat,

he sends out his word on earth
and his word runs quickly,
he gives you snow like wool,
he sprinkles frost like ashes and scatters hail like crumbs of
     ice;
who can stand his coldness?
He sends out his word and melts them,
he makes the wind blow and the water flow
and proves his word to Jacob:
his laws and his judgements to Israel.
He has not done this to any other nation;
they will not know his judgements.
Praise God.

Praise God.
Praise God in the heavens,
praise him in the heights.
Praise him all his angels,
praise him all his armies,
praise him sun and moon,
praise him all stars of light,
praise him heaven of heavens,
and the waters above the heavens.
They shall praise the name of God,
because he commanded
and they were created,
and he set them up to stand for ever and for ever;
he gave them a frontier and they shall not cross it.
Praise God on earth,
sea monsters and all the deep seas,
fire and hail and snow and mist,
stormwind that does his command,
mountains and all hills,
fruit-trees and cedars,
wild beasts and all kinds of cattle,
creeping things and winged birds,
kings of the earth and all peoples, princes and judges of the
    earth,
young men and girls, old men and boys:
they shall praise the name of God,
because his name alone is absolute,
his honour is above the heavens and the earth,

and he has lifted up the horn of his nation,
which is the praise of all his holy ones,
the sons of Israel,
the nation which is close to him.
Praise God.

Praise God.
Sing a new song to God,
his praises in the assembly of saints.
Israel shall be glad with his maker,
the sons of Zion shall praise his name in dancing,
they shall praise him with the music of timbrels and harps.
Because the pleasure of God is his nation,
he shall glorify the poor with freedom,
and the saints shall triumph in glory,
they shall shout with joy on their couches;
the praises of God shall be in their throats
and sharp swords in their hands,
for revenge on the nations and the punishment of peoples
to chain up their kings and to put their chief men in fetter
   of iron,
to execute the judgement which has been written;
and this is the glory of all his saints.
Praise God.

Praise God:
praise him in his holy place,
praise him in the dome of his strength,
praise him in his powers,
praise him in the immensity of his greatness,
praise him with the noise of the horn,
praise him with the lute and the harp,
praise him with timbrels and dancing,
praise him with the pipes and the gong,
praise him with clashing cymbals,
praise him with rejoicing cymbals,
let everything that breathes praise God.
Praise God.

MORE ABOUT PENGUINS
AND PELICANS

For further information about books available from Penguins please write to Dept EP, Penguin Books Ltd, Harmondsworth, Middlesex UB7 0DA.

In the U.S.A.: For a complete list of books available from Penguins in the United States write to Dept DG, Penguin Books, 299 Murray Hill Parkway, East Rutherford, New Jersey 07073.

In Canada: For a complete list of books available from Penguins in Canada write to Penguin Books Canada Ltd, 2801 John Street, Markham, Ontario L3R 1B4.

In Australia: For a complete list of books available from Penguins in Australia write to the Marketing Department, Penguin Books Australia Ltd, P.O. Box 257, Ringwood, Victoria 3134.

In New Zealand: For a complete list of books available from Penguins in New Zealand write to the Marketing Department, Penguin Books (N.Z.) Ltd, Private Bag, Takapuna, Auckland 9.

In India: For a complete list of books available from Penguins in India write to Penguin Overseas Ltd, 706 Eros Apartments, 56 Nehru Place, New Delhi 110019.

CLASSICS IN TRANSLATION
IN PENGUINS

☐ **Remembrance of Things Past** Marcel Proust

☐ Volume One: **Swann's Way, Within a Budding Grove** £7.50
☐ Volume Two: **The Guermantes Way, Cities of the Plain** £7.50
☐ Volume Three: **The Captive, The Fugitive, Time Regained** £7.50

Terence Kilmartin's acclaimed revised version of C. K. Scott Moncrieff's original translation, published in paperback for the first time.

☐ **The Canterbury Tales** Geoffrey Chaucer £2.50

'Every age is a Canterbury Pilgrimage . . . nor can a child be born who is not one of these characters of Chaucer' – William Blake

☐ **Gargantua & Pantagruel** Rabelais £3.95

The fantastic adventures of two giants through which Rabelais (1495–1553) caricatured his life and times in a masterpiece of exuberance and glorious exaggeration.

☐ **The Brothers Karamazov** Fyodor Dostoevsky £3.95

A detective story on many levels, profoundly involving the question of the existence of God, Dostoevsky's great drama of parricide and fraternal jealousy triumphantly fulfilled his aim: 'to find the man in man . . . [to] depict all the depths of the human soul.'

☐ **Fables of Aesop** £1.95

This translation recovers all the old magic of fables in which, too often, the fox steps forward as the cynical hero and a lamb is an ass to lie down with a lion.

☐ **The Three Theban Plays** Sophocles £2.95

A new translation, by Robert Fagles, of *Antigone, Oedipus the King* and *Oedipus at Colonus*, plays all based on the legend of the royal house of Thebes.

CLASSICS IN TRANSLATION
IN PENGUINS

☐ *The Magic Mountain* **Thomas Mann** £3.95

Set in a sanatorium high in the Swiss Alps, this is modern German literature's most spectacular exploration of love and death, and the relationships between them.

☐ *The Good Soldier Švejk* **Jaroslav Hašek** £4.95

The first complete English translation, with illustrations by Josef Lada. 'Hašek was a humorist of the highest calibre . . . A later age will perhaps put him on a level with Cervantes and Rabelais' – Max Brod

These books should be available at all good bookshops or newsagents, but if you live in the UK or the Republic of Ireland and have difficulty in getting to a bookshop, they can be ordered by post. Please indicate the titles required and fill in the form below.

NAME _____ BLOCK CAPITALS

ADDRESS _____

_____

_____

Enclose a cheque or postal order payable to The Penguin Bookshop to cover the total price of books ordered, plus 50p for postage. Readers in the Republic of Ireland should send £1 R equivalent to the sterling prices, plus 67p for postage. Send to: The Penguin Bookshop, 54/56 Bridlesmith Gate, Nottingham, NG1 2GP.

You can also order by phoning (0602) 599295, and quoting your Barclaycard or Access number.

Every effort is made to ensure the accuracy of the price and availability of books at the time of going to press, but it is sometimes necessary to increase prices and in these circumstances retail prices may be shown on the covers of books which may differ from the prices shown in this list or elsewhere. This list is not an offer to supply any book.

This order service is only available to residents in the UK and the Republic of Ireland.

● ● ●